Leap of Faith

THE JOURNEY OF A DREAM: A MEMOIR

Saidah Nairobi

© 2017 Nairobi Enterprises, LLC

All rights reserved. No portion of this book may be used or reproduced in any form without permission except in the case of brief quotations embodied in critical articles and reviews.

Stay connected with me by visiting:
www.saidahnairobi.com

Cover Design by Nairobi Enterprises, LLC
Cover photo by Mason Poole
Back cover photo by Justin Robinson
Interior Design by Penoaks Publishing
Editing by Sherri Lewis

ISBN: 978-0-9986568-0-9

Dedication

This book is dedicated to my wonderful family, friends, and fans. Thank you for being a beautiful reflection of God's love and light. Your energy is a gift and a blessing. I love you.

Contents

INTRODUCTION	1
CHAPTER ONE *The Foundation*	5
CHAPTER TWO *The Dream*	19
CHAPTER THREE *I Am…Part 1: The Process*	35
CHAPTER FOUR *I Am…Part 2: My Crowning Glory*	49
CHAPTER FIVE *I Am…Part 3: The World Tour*	61
CHAPTER SIX *OMG*	71
CHAPTER SEVEN *Mrs. Marvelous*	85
CHAPTER EIGHT *The Dream: Part 2*	99

CHAPTER NINE — 111
Tour Life

CHAPTER TEN — 125
Dream Nuggets

CHAPTER ELEVEN — 141
Formation

ACKNOWLEDGEMENTS — 155

"For the vision is yet for an appointed time; but at the end it will speak, and it will not lie. Though it delays, wait for it; because it will surely come, it will not delay."

—Habakkuk 2:3 KJV

Introduction

"Write the vision. Make it plain."

—Habakkuk 2:2.

IT ALL STARTS WITH A VISION. Vision is defined as the act or power of anticipating that which will or may come to be. I was anticipating a lot of things to come.

I put up my first vision board in December of 2007. I taped positive words of affirmation on my bedroom wall and every time I walked in or out of my room, I looked at those words of affirmation – "I Am Healthy," "I Am Elevating," "I Am Motivated," "I Am Faith-Filled," "I Am Blessed," "I Am Positive," "Money Comes Easily and Frequently," "I Am Successful." I truly believe that visualizing positively helped actualize the manifestation of my goals. Our thoughts do cause the results of our present outcome.

You are what you think and your reality is a reflection of your thoughts. Whatever it is we want to manifest – whether it has to do with relationships, career, finances, spirituality, health, lifestyle desires, etc. – we must visualize and focus only on that which we want. For example, if you want to own your own business and you're tired of working a nine- to-five, don't continue to focus on the fact that you *wish* you weren't at your current job. Instead, focus on the type of business you desire to have.

Every year, and sometimes twice a year, I update my vision board. I firmly believe in the power of our energy. Energy is contagious. Our thoughts are energy, and our focus is energy. If there's anything you want to happen for your life, it starts with a vision.

This is the story of my vision, and ultimately, my journey to being a professional dancer in the mainstream music industry. I wanted to share the story of my dance journey in hopes that it would be a conduit of inspiration to you to always choose to persevere, keep your faith strong, and stay surrounded by encouraging thoughts, people, and ideals. Your dreams can come true.

What should never be an option is giving up on your dreams. If you have a gift, share it. Keeping our gifts to ourselves does us, nor the people who need our gifts, any justice. There's no joy in regret. And to keep saying "what if" would eventually drive you crazy. Don't waste energy on "what if's". Just do it! It's not too late. Begin now. Begin today pursuing your dream full throttle.

If God has placed something on your heart to do, you were destined to do it, and it's not going to leave you. I know this first-hand. The desires of our heart never leave us. We can try to subdue, suppress, or delay our passions, but they will always be there, waiting for us to see them through. Me writing this memoir was a dream. You reading it is the manifestation of that dream. Every word you read in this memoir is a testament to a sound truth…your dreams can manifest into reality. I can do ALL things through Christ that strengthens me – *Philippians 4:13*. This was the first scripture my mother introduced to me as a young girl, and it became the scripture I lived by.

I couldn't ask for better parents. I honor my mother and father for creating the foundation on which I stand. God makes no mistakes. I believe experiences are interconnected, and the journeys my parents trod enabled my evolution, not only as a human being, but as a spirit being. And God has implanted a mountain of inspiration within me that I feel most honored and compelled to share with the world.

Staying positive, staying focused, and keeping the faith even though it's easy to fear the unknown, are key to seeing your dreams come to life. Speak it and so it is. Think it, and so it will be. Ask it and so you shall have. And above all. BELIEVE!

That light that shines in us will guide our path. It all starts with a vision. Here was mine.

CHAPTER ONE

The Foundation

As long as I remember, dance and art were a part of my life. My early years in Queens, and later, Atlanta, provided the perfect foundation for my future as a performer. From my early attempts at break dancing around the house, taking African dance classes in Jamaica, Queens, to my first theater performance at the tender age of six, my mother knew I had an affinity for the arts and sought out ways to nurture it. Once we moved down south, my exposure to southern music and culture further expanded my love.

Some of my fondest memories growing up in Atlanta were going to the skating rink and jamming to the latest hot records. Back in the 90's, there was plenty of new music from the "dirty south" to skate to like, "Tootsie Roll", "Shawty Swing My Way", "Whatz Up, Whatz Up", "Da Dip", and "Scrub da Ground." ATL was HOT on the music scene, too. We had artists like TLC, Usher, and OutKast breaking out, and the dopest labels at the time were based in ATL. So So Def and LaFace Records were dominating the airwaves!

Being involved in my church growing up contributed to my faith and this growing love I had for outlets of expression. The worship service in my southern Baptist church was full of power and passion and gave me my first experiences with praise dancing and singing in a choir.

In elementary school, I cultivated my musical skills by taking chorus and band classes. I played clarinet until I briefly relocated to Brooklyn, where I took theater classes at MS 113.

By the time I reached the 8th grade, I was able to enroll in a performing arts high school in Atlanta – DeKalb School of the Arts – the greatest school ever and the best gift of my teenage years. DSA was a small performing arts school full of dancers, singers, musicians, actors, techies, and media enthusiasts. Our days were structured with a delicate balance between academic and arts classes. After school, there were a number of extracurricular activities for students to be involved in, from show choirs to gospel choirs, dance repertoire companies to musical productions. We were a student body full of creative expression and expansion, in other words, nerdy and artsy kids!

Notable DSA alumni include R&B singer Lloyd and actor/rapper Donald Glover also known as Childish Gambino.

Talent was everywhere! You'd find dancers doing leaps up and down the hallways, vocalists singing in groups during lunch break, musicians outside playing the guitar, thespians acting out parts for school musicals – all types of creative channels, all day long. Between my schedule for classes and various organizations I was a member of, I would leave for school at six in the morning and sometimes didn't get home until eight o'clock at night.

I auditioned for entry into DSA by playing the clarinet and performing a monologue. I started out as a band major, theater minor. By my sophomore year, I ended up becoming a vocal major, dance minor. I loved everything about the arts, so I wanted to do it all. Sing, dance, act, and play in the concert band. The great thing about DSA was that we had the freedom and flexibility to explore all the departments the school had to offer.

Ultimately, music and dance became my sole focuses at DSA. But my focus was limited in dance because I was only passionate about African, hip-hop, and yeek dancing. Yeeking was an Atlanta-based, high-energy style of dance that popularized in the 90s. I appreciated jazz and tap but I couldn't, for the life of me, understand or relate to the techniques of ballet or modern dancing, and consequently didn't take those styles of dance seriously. I was more interested in learning about the history of yeeking, or the history of hip-hop dance and African dance instead of learning how to *tendu*.

Both at DSA and McClendon School of Dance – an excellent black-owned dance school in Atlanta that I briefly trained at – I didn't take the technical classes available seriously. I just wanted to move to music that I liked and listened to. At the time, I didn't realize that praise dancing correlated with modern, jazz, and ballet technique, but when I freestyled to worship music in church, movement that I learned from those classes would naturally come out.

I wish I'd understood the long-term importance of ballet and modern classes back then. No one explained exactly why those classes would be important for my future as a dancer. I thought they were pointless – like algebra. I wasn't convinced that I was going to apply "xy+2z=whatever" to my life as an adult. So unfortunately, I didn't take full advantage of the opportunity to perfect my craft as a dancer at a young age.

As I got older, I learned the importance of those styles of dance for the overall longevity, flexibility, and versatility of a dancer. But being the highly opinionated and passionate young girl I was, and having no shame in staying true to my specific interests, I was all about dancing to music that made me groove. And hip-hop, African, and yeeking were some of the only styles of dancing where I felt that groove.

My sophomore year of high school, I auditioned for and joined the only all-girl, hip-hop dance squad from our school, Isis Gold. Similar to what competition dance is in the studio company world, high school talent shows were the main event street dance squads prepared for in Atlanta. Every year, we looked forward to showcasing our originality because Isis Gold was THE best female dance squad in ATL. Our moves contained a mixture of yeeking, hip-hop, and what we called, "hood sexy". We were feminine even though we danced aggressive, like dudes. Being in Isis Gold created the foundation for my early style of dance.

If any of you reading this book go to a performing arts school, PLEASE take FULL advantage of each and every class available. If you love to sing, take piano class, take guitar lessons, and join the band, because you may realize that you want to play an instrument as an artist later. Take full advantage of choir classes. They perfect your skills in harmonization. Take the vocal lessons. Learn to read music.

Participate in every recital and production and talent show and showcase you possibly can. This will increase your confidence, creativity and experience as a performer. You'll understand more what it takes to put together a production. Join the tech classes. They may be boring, but if you're trying to be an actor, a musician, an artist, techies are crucial to the success of a production. It helps when you understand their world.

Take EVERY dance class you can take. Ballet is very important for posture, for your lines and helps keep your muscles limber. It increases your awareness of what your body is doing and how it looks when you do certain movements. The more classes you take in ballet, hip hop, modern, tap, jazz, the more equipped you are to finesse every style of dance and ultimately create your own style in the midst of all the techniques you have. The sky's the limit when you're a proficient dancer in all areas of dance.

Take the acting classes. Audition. Audition. Audition. You'll be doing a lot of it to become a professional. Might as well get used to the experience of it.

Even if you're not sure what part of the arts you want to ultimately pursue, if you have a passion for the arts, then take your passion seriously. It's better to be prepared than to have to get prepared when you figure out what you want to do.

In my senior year of high school at DSA, I was feeling those bittersweet emotions anticipating departing from the safe confinements of the artistic and academic environment I had come to know and love.

My dream college was New York University's Tisch School of the Arts, but the annual tuition there was overwhelmingly high. Instead, I set my sights on a historically black college in Greensboro, NC – Bennett College for Women. My sister was living in Greensboro at the time – which was a major bonus – but I was also attracted to the small population of the school because that meant intimate classroom settings.

I also loved the historical energy and atmosphere of the campus, the quality and value of sisterhood, and that good ol' southern, down-to-earth hospitality and warmth Bennett provided.

In the summer of 2004, I prepared to leave the nest and attend Bennett College as a "freshwoman." I received the schedule for the New Student Orientation in the mail and immediately my eyes zoomed in to the words "Freshwomen Talent Show." The first thing that came to mind was, "I *have* to *dance*." It seemed like from out of nowhere, I gained this courage of sorts. I wanted to be known at Bennett as Saidah the Dancer and to share a piece of who I was with my new family. So I signed up for what would be my FIRST time dancing on stage, all by myself.

I choreographed a routine and put together a mix of some of my favorite songs for the talent show. The adrenaline flowed through my body as I danced and when I finished performing at the Little Theater at Bennett College, I had a standing ovation. It felt incredible! Although I wasn't attending my performing arts high school anymore, I wanted dance to be a part of my life WHEREVER I went.

About a month later, in September, one of my fellow Bennett sisters eagerly approached me to announce that there were auditions the following night for the dance sector of Couture Productions – a college organization at our neighboring university, North Carolina A&T.

I only had thirty seconds to show them what I was made of, so I chose to dance to "Beat It" by Michael Jackson. I remember sitting in the audition room, nervous as ever! A&T was a much bigger campus – intimidating compared to how calm and laid back things were at Bennett. I felt as if I'd stepped into a university for real. I was with the big dogs! What if they booed me?

I was STILL trying to figure out, "What am I going to do for the VERY beginning intro to "Beat It?" I had no clue. There I was sitting, time just ticking away, my name could be called any minute, and with only thirty seconds to impress, I didn't know what to do with the first ten seconds!

Then, flashing back to a signature move we had done in Isis Gold called, "The Matrix", a light bulb came on in my head! *Ting!* That would be perfect! For the first gong that goes off in the intro to "Beat It", I would fall back into the matrix, next gong, lean to the left, next gong, lean back to center. Next gong, lean to the right, next gong come back center. And for the last gong, drop even lower in the matrix. It seemed brilliant!

And it was. I wore these pink velour pants, no shoes, white socks, and a white tank top. And as soon as the first "gong" kicked in, I bent all the way backwards with my arms out to the side and the room ERUPTED! I had JUST started!

By the time I finished, I had yet another standing ovation. They were going crazy for me! I was relieved and ecstatic. This wasn't even my "turf" and I was getting so much love! That same night, I got a call from "Byrd", who would later become one of my best friends, saying, "Congratulations, you've been selected to go through Hell Week for the dance sector of Couture Productions."

I didn't know what in the world hell week meant, but I was on a cloud! Hell Week turned out to be a weeklong, intense audition process where we learned choreography, worked out, and had freestyle battles every day. At the end of the week, the organization would make a final decision on who made it into Couture. Who knew that this college organization was actually preparing me for a real life, professional experience four years later?

Dancing was only a hobby for me when I entered college. Although I'd spent four and a half years at a performing arts high school, I had no solid aspirations to be an entertainer.

The way I was taught, getting a college degree was inevitable, but I was always changing my mind about what I wanted to be. At one time or another, my career aspirations were to be a teacher, a civil litigator, an obstetrician, a psychologist, a sociologist, a marriage counselor, a guidance counselor, a superintendent, and even a neonatal nurse. Out of all these careers, I went to college to pursue a degree in Education to become a middle or high school English teacher.

English was my FAVORITE subject in school. I've always loved writing, reading, and literature. But when I went to a teaching seminar my second semester, something hit me and it hit me strong. I knew there was something I was truly passionate about that I could see myself doing for a LONG time, but it wasn't being an English teacher. I had to figure it out. What did I want to do?

Second semester of my freshman year, I wasn't fully active with Couture Productions, because I started working part-time at Applebee's. But I truly missed dancing. It hurt going to Couture's rehearsals and just watching because I couldn't participate. I missed too many rehearsals. I eventually stopped working and returned to Couture, but by that time, me and a few of the members had created a separate dance crew – a smaller, more intensely focused group of dancers called HipHopcrisy. This select group of dancers had serious talent and a burning passion for dance.

It was HipHopcrisy that birthed the inspiration for me to pursue a career in dance. If it weren't for this crew and the special connection that me and my friends Byrd, Donald, and Clifton shared in it, my journey would have been a lot different. We were like the Three Musketeers, except there were four of us – an inseparable group of friends. Dancing was the first and last thing we did every day. We genuinely enjoyed training together and breathing life into our passion. Together.

By mid-summer 2005, I was torn between continuing my education at Bennett College and moving back to Georgia. I was awarded a full-tuition scholarship for my first year at Bennett, but when I saw how much it would cost my second year, it was unnerving. My thought was, if I'm going to invest so much time and money into something, I'd better love what I'm investing in with all my heart. I didn't love being an Education major with all my heart. But there was one thing I did love. Dancing.

Therefore, at the end of my first year at Bennett College, I packed up all of my belongings in my dorm room and moved into my friend Byrd's townhome off campus. I stayed in Greensboro, NC for the entire summer just so I could dance. Besides the summers I spent with my father in Brooklyn, this was the best summer of my youth. My sister lived in Greensboro at the time too, so I was able to spend quality time with her in addition to dancing.

All summer long, HipHopcrisy spent countless hours rehearsing to perform wherever we could throughout the state of North Carolina. We were HUNGRY. We were MOTIVATED. We just wanted to dance and perform.

We spent hours mixing our own music, making up our own steps, coordinating our own wardrobe and looks – all because we loved what we did.

Most of the time, we barely had two pennies to rub together. Little Caesar's Pizza, frozen dollar pizzas from Harris Teeter's, McDonalds, and George Foreman grilled hot dogs were my regular meals for the summer. We didn't make a dime off of rehearsing and performing, but we had the deepest gratitude in our hearts. For each other, for our passions, and for the dreams we hoped to one day make a reality.

Meaningful and sincere friendships are so important. The best thing you can do for your future and the realization of your dreams is to surround yourself with positive motivators.

We spent hours upon hours watching Usher's "Truth" Tour, Janet Jackson's "All For You" Tour, and any and every video that had choreography in it. From Aaliyah, Omarion, Ciara, J.Lo, and Janet, to Britney, Destiny's Child, Sean Paul, and Missy Elliot – we knew the names of every dancer and choreographer for these artists. We studied hard.

By the end of summer '05, my decision was clear. I was moving back to Atlanta. When I saw Ciara's music videos "Goodies", "1,2 Step", and "Oh", it clicked. I saw this tall girl getting low to the ground, serving attitude and that unique southern flair, and I looked at those dance steps in the videos and said, "Yo! That's me all day! That's ATL all day!"

Watching Ciara and her dancers do the matrix in the "Goodies" video reminded me of dancing in high school with my girls in Isis Gold. The grooves in those videos spoke my very language. I researched the choreographer for Ciara, found out her name was Jamaica Craft, and that's what propelled me to pursue dancing professionally. To dance those same grooves right alongside Ciara one day was my goal. And I wasn't giving my dream up for anything.

> *"For I know the plans I have for you. Plans to prosper you, not to harm you. Plans to give you hope and a future".*
>
> —Jeremiah 29:11

Lessons From The Foundation

- The signs are all there from our youth as to what we are naturally drawn to. The best thing a parent can do is recognize these signs, and cultivate and nurture their child's interests.

- Whatever we are passionate about, it is necessary to understand the fundamental structure and history behind it. It may not make sense in the present, but it will in the future.

- The purpose of a foundation is to be the root for greater building. Take the groundwork seriously so whatever is built on it will stand.

Chapter Two

The Dream

In the fall of 2005, I was back in ATL, attending school online, working, and taking dance classes at a studio called Gotta Dance Atlanta. I also discovered a talent agency named Two8Counts that signed me.

Things were flowing smoothly. Shortly after signing with Two8Counts, I booked my first ever paying dance gig as a freestyle dancer. It was for the music video of Atlanta rappers, G-Dinero and Pastor Troy, for their new song, "Tilt Your Hat."

The set for the video was at the house of former boxing champion, Evander Holyfield. That was so random to me. But music video sets can be random in general. You would never know that there were only ten people on set for a "club scene," which wasn't shot at an actual club, but a warehouse. On television though, it looks like the "club" is popping and a fire marshal would be coming to shut it down at any moment!

I was nervous, but excited as I pulled up to the gate. I was in heavy observation mode the entire day. I watched everything from the artists, to the principle and background talent, to the models, the entourage, the producers, director, and production assistants. Witnessing for the first time the number of long hours put into a music video shoot was an eye-opening experience.

As we sat in Evander Holyfield's garage, which was the holding area for background talent, I could tell it wasn't the first video shoot for most of the other talent because they had their hair and makeup products handy. I, on the other hand, came with neither. I heard of hair and make-up departments on sets, so I assumed there would be hair and make-up stylists for us. Not so much. I had a lot to learn! At the end of the shoot, also known as wrap, I was given $50 cash in a white envelope by my agent. I was able to drive home from set with a full tank of gas and a happy meal.

By January 2006, I was attending Georgia State University part-time and living in student housing off-campus. I was trying to keep my mother happy by going to school, but I was getting called on more and more auditions, and slowly but surely, school became secondary.

I was missing classes and tests. But I wasn't missing auditions, nor was I missing rehearsals with IMD.

IMD – Infinite Movement Dance – was a new boutique company I was dancing with. Under the direction of Gee Gee Ibarra, IMD performed at any event we could in the metro Atlanta area.

The energy was fresh at IMD, because we were all hungry to dance and each had uniquely different backgrounds that brought us to Atlanta and to that tiny, little known dance studio on Auburn Avenue. I also developed close friendships with three of the members – Chi Chi, JaQuez, and Jonathan – who were equally serious about making a profession out of dance. We played key roles in being each other's support system over the years. With the disbandment of my former crew, HipHopcrisy – everyone had spread out to different cities. It was motivating to be a part of a new team.

I officially dropped out of college in spring of 2006. I knew where my heart was, and I was ready to go for it. Withdrawing from school meant I had no degree to "fall back on," so failure was not an option. Since I had to move out of campus housing, and it wasn't an option to move back home, I had to find a place to live.

Byrd, being the good friend she always was, asked her cousin if I could move in with her and split the rent and bills. She had a spare bedroom and could use the help with rent, so she agreed. I was working a part-time job at a children's play place called Monkey Joes, and by the fall, I got promoted to the General Manager position. I was only nineteen years old.

Being responsible for the management of a facility, overseeing fifteen to twenty employees, and having three bosses wasn't easy. I didn't take for granted that the owners trusted me to manage their business at such a young age, so I embraced the responsibilities and took my job seriously.

During the day I managed Monkey Joes, and on weekend nights, I was go-go dancing in Atlanta nightclubs. Go-go dancing is not to be confused with stripping. Our job was to keep up the energy in the club as we danced to every song the DJ spun. We usually wore color-coordinated outfits or costume themes for the shifts. We were always elevated above the dance floor on go-go boxes so all eyes could be on us.

I would let the music move me as the DJ went from one song to the next to the next. At some clubs, it was boring dancing for hours, because either the music wasn't of my taste, or there wasn't much of a crowd. I go-go danced for almost two years, and it was a fun gig to have that also helped me become better at freestyling. Plus, it was a great hustle that ensured I had extra money every month after bills were paid. I was still far from what I dreamed for, but I respected the journey getting there.

In order to grow, sometimes decisions have to be made that cause us to step outside of our comfort zones. The decisions may not come easy, and they may be scary even, because of fear of the unknown. By Spring 2007, I felt it was time to make such a decision. May 15, 2007 was my last day as General Manager at Monkey Joes and my last day on any payroll unrelated to the arts. I decided if I was going to become a professional dancer, I had to move in faith and commit to my pursuit full-time.

My bosses at Monkey Joes didn't want to see me go, but they wanted to see me grow. They respected my decision to leave my management position to pursue what I truly loved. I affirmed to myself that dancing was going to be my bread and butter. I didn't know how, but I knew that it would be. I was faith-filled and trusting that God was guiding my path.

A few months later, I ended my two-year relationship with my dance agent, Two8Counts. An agent is not supposed to do all the work for your career, but there should be a high level of confidence that you're in an exclusive agreement with an agent that understands, respects, and supports your career goals, believes in you, fights for you, and works hard to ensure your success.

I found these qualities in a new talent agent that had emerged in Atlanta by the name of Aris Golemi. In the fall of 2007, I signed with his boutique agency, Xcel Talent.

It had been two years since I made my decision to move to Atlanta and I hadn't made my first break yet. Professional opportunities were so close, yet so far away in this period. I had auditioned twice for Beyoncé's choreographer at the time, Frank Gatson – one for a series of music videos Beyoncé was shooting for her album B'Day, and another for a gig with R&B singer Monica. I had also auditioned for the choreographer of my dreams, Jamaica Craft, for Ciara's music video, "That's Right," as well as at a private agency audition for talent scouting. But those opportunities came and went.

In spite of not landing those jobs, I wasn't discouraged and it was fueling my hunger that much more. I needed to be ripe and refined. I continued to remind myself that everything is about timing and I believed that things would soon look up. So I kept on grinding. Even though I couldn't see when my break was coming, I knew the opportunity I had been working for required my diligence and patience.

> *"But if we hope for what we do not yet have, we wait for it patiently."*
>
> *—Romans 8:25*

It behooves one to be a flexible person in this industry, because new opportunities are subject to pop up at any given moment and they require a quick yes or a quick no. Either you want it or you don't and there's little to no room to think about it. As Bruce Lee once said, "Don't think, just feel."

I continued to book as either a feature talent or freestyle dancer in a number of music videos until I got a call late one night from my good friend, Chi Chi, who was beginning to work as a choreographer in the industry. She needed four principle dancers for a new music video by Rick Ross featuring R. Kelly called "Speedin."

I told her I was available to do it and within a few hours, we were at the dance studio learning and rehearsing the choreography for the shoot. Shortly after rehearsal – which was at around 5 in the morning – we were in a van driving from Atlanta to Miami to shoot the video. Once we got to Miami, we were literally scrambling around at shopping outlets looking for wardrobe for the video moments before we had to shoot.

This opportunity proved to be the signal of a turning point.

It was now Spring 2008. If I had stayed in college full-time, I would have been a part of the graduating class of 2008 with an undergrad degree under my belt. Instead, I was at Complex Studios in Atlanta, GA auditioning for a national tour. This would be my very first opportunity at touring as a dancer. The artist's name? The Dream.

Very befitting. The tour? Mary J. Blige and Jay-Z's "Heart of the City" Tour. The choreographer? Jamaica Craft.

The Dream would be the opening act for the tour. The idea of being able to watch two of my all-time favorite artists perform every night for two months was thrilling. So was the idea of getting consistent pay for at least two months. But most importantly, to work with Jamaica Craft would be the beginning of a dream realized. All I needed – all I wanted so badly – was the opportunity for her to see what I could do.

One of the important things to understand about this industry is that it's all about who knows YOU. It's not about who YOU know. You could know the name of every choreographer that hires dancers for all of the major artists in the U.S., but if these choreographers don't know your name or what you look like, it doesn't mean a thing.

I knew about Jamaica Craft three years before she ever knew who I was, and it took her seeing me three times before she would finally see that spark in me.

At the tour audition, we were brought into the room one at a time to freestyle after we learned the routine from Jamaica's assistant, Oththan Burnside. Oththan also happened to be one of my favorite dancers, so learning from her was a treat. When it came time to freestyle, I knew it was do or die, and I blacked all the way out. In the middle of my freestyle I heard Jamaica yell, "There it is! That's it!" At last. I was ripe and ready.

The following night, I got the call that I had been booked for one of the four spots available on the tour. Less than one year after stepping out on faith and declaring dance as my bread and butter, I was officially booked on my first tour and getting a salary as a professional dancer.

Although I didn't have a college degree, I was making my dream come true. My friends and family were overjoyed for me. They knew I wouldn't quit on my dream and my perseverance became a source of inspiration and a testimony to those near and dear to me. It took two and a half years, but the time had come. And I was beyond grateful.

Being on the road for the first time was unforgettable. Visiting cities I had never been to before, from Los Angeles to Las Vegas, to performing in my hometown of Atlanta at the Philips Arena, gave me a type of rush I'd never felt. There is something so magical about performing at Madison Square Garden in New York City, and we did it three times on "The Heart of the City" Tour. I had been to concerts before I went on this tour, but the amount of energy and the volume of the screams from the audience at Madison Square Garden, is on another level.

During the tour, The Dream was scheduled to shoot a music video for his new single, "I Luv Your Girl." Four of the eight dancers hired for the music video were already in rehearsals with Jamaica, so as soon as me and the other tour dancers arrived in Atlanta, we headed to straight to rehearsal. The shoot would be the next day, so everything was happening quickly.

On the day of the video shoot, there were a lot of celebrity music artists on set, but there was one artist in particular that I saw watching in the corner as we shot our dance sequence – Ciara. I was being so cool on the outside, but inside I was doing cartwheels! Ciara was watching ME dance! I was given an opportunity for Ciara to see how I groove and perform.

My hope was that she would be like, "Jamaica! I want her! She's dancing with me!"

I didn't have to hope long.

It was summer of 2008 and the tour had ended as my first major feature in a video had debuted. Friends and family were calling me left and right, screaming excitedly that they saw me in The Dream's new video and how they were so proud of me. It was an amazing feeling to make my friends and family proud and be a testament that chasing your dreams will not go in vain if you believe with all of your heart that what you set your mind to achieving will happen.

It wasn't long after the video premiere that the call I had been waiting for finally came! Jamaica wanted to book me to dance with Ciara in Nelly featuring her and Jermaine Dupri's new music video, "Stepped on My J's."

What! I'm going to get to dance with Ciara?!

I wanted to cry. I did cry. What a testimony. My dream had actually come true. Three summers after I moved back to Atlanta and made the decision to become a professional dancer, here I was, in rehearsals with the very women who inspired my dream – Ciara and Jamaica Craft.

I didn't know what to do with myself but thank God over and over.

It was surreal. I was seeing the dream come to life. I had so much fun shooting the music video for "Stepped on my J's." Our first shot was just us girls pulling up to the party in a Cadillac. We stepped out the car and then busted into the choreography, which was fun, flirty, and swagged out. It was also my first time rocking a pair of Jordan's, which we got to keep!

Ciara was everything I thought she would be. Cool, chill, sweet, goofy, and fun to work with. I had one of the best phone conversations with my best friend, Donald, when I shared the news with him. It brought him to tears. It gave us so much assurance to believe in our dreams and be faith-filled that God will bring to life the desires of our hearts and the visions and goals we set. When your heart is in the right place, your dreams are unstoppable.

My work as a dancer seemed to be in domino effect. I flew to LA to perform for the first time on an award show – the 2008 BET Awards – for the song, "Stepped on my J's."

My mom, dad, sister, and my baby brother were going to see me perform live on television! It was a special moment because I was experiencing so many firsts in my career. My first tour, my first time working with Jamaica Craft, my first gig dancing with Ciara, my first award show performance. Just a year before, it was all a dream – I was jobless and aspiring to be a professional dancer. One year later, I'm dancing next to Ciara on stage in Los Angeles for the BET Awards.

Working with Ciara continued with rehearsals for her "Fantasy Ride" promotional tour, which was slated for fall of 2008. For this job, I got the opportunity to dance alongside the very woman who auditioned me for The Dream – Oththan Burnside. As an aspiring dancer, I had studied and admired her because she had this aggressive, electric fire and energy about her when she danced and it was so easy to identify her amongst even twenty girls on the same stage. It was an honor.

I also got to learn and perform the official choreography to, "Goodies", "Oh", and "1,2 Step." Only four years ago, I was watching those videos over and over again so I could learn the choreography. Then when I'd go to the club and Ciara's songs came on, I would clear the dance floor so I could bust out doing all the choreography from the videos. Like I was one of the dancers.

We were prepared to do a number of shows and me and my passport were ready to hit the road, but unfortunately, after one concert, the promotional tour was cancelled.

A few months later, in January 2009, we were back in rehearsals for the music video to Ciara's new single, "Never Ever." Little did I know, my journey was getting ready to head in a completely new direction.

After two music videos, one award show, and a concert performance with my dream artist, it would be a while before I'd work with Ciara again.

Lessons From The Dream

- Focus on WHAT you want to achieve. Don't worry about the HOW. I knew I wanted to work with Jamaica Craft and that I wanted to dance for Ciara, but I didn't know how those opportunities were going to come to pass. I certainly couldn't have predicted that my first opportunity to work for Jamaica would be dancing for The Dream.

  And I certainly couldn't have predicted that my first opportunity to dance for Ciara would be in a music video for a song she recorded with Nelly and Jermaine Dupri. We're not capable of knowing the exact path, channel, or door that will ultimately lead to achieving our goals. But God knows. God beholds the pathways to infinite possibilities. And if you keep your faith strong, the burden of the unknown will become the joy of certainty. Because you'll believe and know without a doubt, that what you dream will come to be.

- Life can turn around at any given moment. If we believe in thegood, endure the waiting period, and let nothing discourage us from pursuing our purpose in life, good things will begin to happen.

- Patience, hard work, and faith go a long way. The desires of our hearts will eventually come to pass in some form, shape, or fashion. Guaranteed. What's not guaranteed is that it'll happen when YOU want it to happen. But it will happen exactly when it's supposed to. Timing is everything.

Chapter Three

I Am... Part 1:

The Process

"Congratulations, Saidah. You are one of the six girls selected that will continue auditioning this week for one of the four spots on Beyoncé's tour. We've never worked with you before, but we like you, so we want to see what you can do. See you tomorrow."

This was choreographer, Frank Gatson, speaking to me over the phone. It was the night of February 2, 2009. I will never forget this date, nor this phone call, because my dance career, as I knew it, was officially taking off on a whole new level.

Let me rewind to the morning of February 2, 2009. I had just flown in to New York for a live performance with Keri Hilson – a new R&B singer/songwriter Jamaica Craft hired me to dance for – on *106&Park*. This gig happened to be on the same day and in the same city as the callback auditions for Beyoncé's upcoming world tour. I missed the first auditions in November because I was in rehearsals with Ciara for her "Fantasy Ride" promo tour. But my agent asked Frank Gatson if I could attend the callback auditions, and Frank obliged.

As fate would have it, I ended up being in New York right on time for this opportunity. However, the callbacks were starting at 3pm. At that time, I was doing camera blocking for the live taping of Keri's performance and *106&Park* didn't go live until 6pm. Nerves were a little high because I was already missing three hours of the audition.

We didn't perform on *106&Park* until about 7:30pm. I just knew the auditions were over. Four and a half hours later and I'm trying to show up to callback auditions for Beyoncé's tour? Impossible.

The dancer I was doing the Keri Hilson gig with, Neo, was invited to the callback auditions as well, so we were both looking at the clock and looking at each other like, "What are we going to do? Can we still make it?"

We called our agent, Aris, and he urged us saying, "Go, go! It's not too late, they're still there!"

We threw our all black on, put on our heels, and hopped in a cab. And what do you know? Alvin Ailey Dance Theater, where the callbacks were being held, was two blocks from where we were taping *106&Park*. Could that have worked out any more perfectly?

We arrived shortly before 8p.m. I was prepared to just give Frank Gatson my headshot in hopes that he would consider me for something in the future.

When we walked in, the last group of girls was completing their audition. To my astonishment, everyone was still there – including Beyoncé. We tiptoed over to Frank with our headshots. I knew there was no way they were going to let us walk in five hours late and audition.

To my surprise, Frank looked at us and asked, "Do y'all know 'Single Ladies'?"

We vigorously nodded our heads. Prior to us arriving in New York, Neo had taught me the "Single Ladies" routine she'd learned from the first auditions.

Frank said, "Well all right, let's see it."

The other girls auditioning cleared the floor and right there on the spot, me and Neo, who just not even half an hour ago got off stage with Keri Hilson, danced the "Single Ladies" routine before Frank Gatson, JaQuel Knight, and Beyoncé herself. The remaining girls in the audition room cheered us on as we performed. I later found out that I was doing that dance strong, but wrong. I didn't realize how watered down I was doing the "Single

Ladies" dance, but once I properly learned the routine, I shook my head thinking, "How in the WORLD did I manage to get on this tour?"

I know it was a question a LOT of girls who auditioned for the tour were asking. For one, I was a brand new face to practically everyone in that room. And I was beyond late. The auditions were pretty much over! And I didn't even attend the initial auditions for the tour! But what God has for you is for you. Nobody can get in the way of where God wants you to be. I truly believe that my experience getting on Beyoncé's 2009-2010 *I Am...* World Tour was a direct reflection of that.

After we finished performing our rendition of "Single Ladies," Frank released the girls that had been auditioning all day, and told me and Neo to stay. Frank then had JaQuel teach us part of the routine to "Naughty Girl." After we learned and performed that song, Frank had us learn, "Crazy in Love."

Before I did the "Single Ladies" routine at the audition, Frank asked me if I was trained. I told him, "No, I'm not professionally trained, I just love dance. I'm a raw dancer."

So for the "Crazy in Love" segment of our audition, it was all about Frank seeing if I knew my lines. He wanted to see if I knew how to bevel my legs, if I knew how to walk and stand like a grown, confident, commanding woman. A woman like Beyoncé.

He had us do a variation of jazz lines to see if I could at least handle the basics. To my complete amazement and deepest appreciation, Beyoncé sat there in front of us and watched.

The. Entire. Time.

She could've left after the girls that had been there since 3pm left, but she was there. Even though Neo and I were the ones who were late, she gave us a fair chance and watched us go through our audition process. That spoke major volumes to me. I was wowed and I deeply respect Beyoncé for doing that.

The following afternoon, February 3, 2009, I was on the 6th floor of the Alvin Ailey Dance Theater to begin rehearsals and continue the audition process for Beyoncé's tour. Earlier that day, I'd made a mad dash for a clothing store to purchase as many leggings and tops as I could find to last me the week. I only had an overnight bag with me and practically no clothes because I was expecting to catch a 5am flight back to Atlanta that morning.

But instead, by God's divine design, I was checking out of the hotel I had reserved for one night, and moving into my very own one-bedroom apartment at the Blake. Every dancer from out of town was housed in these apartments. It was an amazing blessing for everyone to be housed in individual apartments because they could've had two dancers per apartment.

At our first rehearsal, I had a lot of choreography to catch up on. Besides "Single Ladies," the other five female dancers knew the entire combination to "Naughty Girl," because they were taught it at the callbacks. I was only taught a small portion of it at the callbacks, so while JaQuel was going over "Naughty Girl" with the other girls, Chris Grant – Frank's assistant choreographer – was with me in the corner teaching me the rest of the routine. The same Chris Grant who would, two months later, become one of Michael Jackson's dancers for his "This Is It" Tour and a few years later, become Beyoncé's head choreographer.

A week passed. All six female dancers were still there. We were being placed in formations as if all six of us were going on tour and things were moving along at a swift pace as we learned two to three numbers a day.

Soon, I learned that a tennis ball would be the greatest friend to my feet. This was my first experience being in eight to ten hour rehearsals dancing only in heels. Dancing in heels is flat out sexy and came with being on tour with an artist like Beyoncé. We grinned and bore it – the early mornings and late nights. We were all tirelessly working hard. We were still unsure of who would ultimately be the four girls to go on tour, but we each did our absolute best to secure our spot.

One particular evening, we all had to take turns doing each of the dance numbers we had learned so far in pairs. Beyoncé sat in front of the mirror watching the entire time. This was something we hadn't done before, so we all knew this was a do-or-die situation – the moment of initiation or elimination.

Everyone was going full out, dancing with everything they had. We all wanted it so bad. To be so close, rehearsing every day for almost two weeks and to then be eliminated was not an option.

I could've screamed when, during one of the numbers, one of my heels broke! I was floored as to why this would happen in this exact moment, but I wasn't going to let a broken heel stop me. I kept dancing anyway.

The next morning, something was different. For about a good hour, we figured one of the dancers was running late. But once rehearsal began, and none of the choreographers asked where she was, we knew it meant only one thing. There were now five girls left.

We didn't want anyone else to get cut. We had grown attached to one another, supporting each other throughout the experience, because even though we were all competing with each other, we became friends in the process. Although it was an odd number with five girls, something felt right about me, Tanee McCall, Kimberly Gipson, Ashley Everett, and Ashley Seldon being together. Dancing together. We were determined to show and prove to Frank, JaQuel, and Beyoncé that the five of us belonged together on this tour.

I guess they felt the magic too, because after three weeks of being on pins and needles, speculating, and praying, we received the official congratulatory announcement that we were all booked to go on Beyoncé's *I Am…* World Tour.

The first round of congratulations was a tease, thanks to JaQuel. He came in to rehearsal, happy as pie, saying, "Congratulations, Ladies!"

We were like, "Congratulations? For what?"

He said, "Oh, oh. Uh, never mind then. I take it back."

We were so distraught like, "Awww man! Nooooo! Don't tease us like that!"

Our agents hadn't contacted us yet about being officially booked for the tour, but I guess JaQuel already knew it was a done deal. Finally that evening, one by one, we all started getting texts from our agents about the good news. We were so relieved and happy! God is so good! This was going to be an amazing journey!

Initially, I didn't think they knew what to do with me. To be honest, I felt like I had no definitive opposite for the tour. Ashley Everett and Kimmie were a perfect match. Ashley Seldon and Tanee were also a perfect match. Then there was me.

Throughout the rehearsal process, I wondered where I fit in. During one rehearsal, Frank pulled me and Tanee aside, explaining that we were going to be mannequins for the tour.

Because of our bodies, the mannequin concept the costume designer for the tour, Thierry Muglier, had envisioned worked great for us. I didn't know if that meant I wouldn't be dancing at all, or if I would only be in certain numbers. I hoped to God I would still get to be a part of at least some of the routines I'd learn. I would've been grateful even if I was only going to be a mannequin, but to have spent so much time and energy learning and perfecting all of the dances, only to be in none would've been heart-breaking.

A few days after receiving the good news on booking the tour, we all flew out to LA to tape video content for the show. The female dancers were going to do a dance medley and the video content was the intro to our medley.

In LA, we, at last, met the male dancers who would also be on tour with us; Cassidy Noblett, Bryan Tanaka, Khasan Brailsford, and Shaun Walker. This would be my first time working on a professional job with male dancers, and being on a tour with nine dancers. This would be my team for the next year.

All of the tour dancers were in LA to also learn a contemporary dance number to Beyoncé's song, "Scared of Lonely." This proved to be the most difficult part of the entire rehearsal process for me because I was not considered a trained dancer. I loved the choreography and wanted to do that number so bad. It was a beautiful partner piece. I learned it and executed it to the best of my ability in rehearsal, but I was frustrated to not to be able to execute it at the level of grace, ease, and effortlessness that I would've been able to if I had the proper training. But I embraced and enjoyed the challenge of taking in a different style of choreography.

Once we were all back in New York, we only had a few more days of dance rehearsals left before it was time to go into production rehearsals. Production rehearsals include all the elements of tour – the dancers, band, singers, crew, lighting, costumes, music, the stage, and most importantly, the artist – Beyoncé.

Everyone was mostly aware of what numbers we were and weren't going to dance in, but one of the last numbers still open was "Single Ladies." Ashley Everett was definitely dancing in that number, but it was undecided who the other girl would be.

Production rehearsals are the time for every department to get the final kinks out before opening night. I will never forget our very first dress rehearsal for the tour. All of the female dancers had tried on their costumes for the opening number, "Crazy in Love" – shiny, leather, solid-colored corsets with leather pants, one in red, one in white, one in black, and one in silver.

All five of the female dancers were performing in the opening number, but there were only four, leather outfits.

Because of the original concept, wardrobe only had two costumes for me – but both were gold mannequin/robot suits. One was a full, head-to-toe suit for the dance numbers, "Diva" and "Radio." The second was a sexier mannequin/robot suit that didn't cover my face.

I still had no wardrobe for the opening number that would also flow into "Naughty Girl," followed by "Freakum Dress." On day one of dress rehearsal, I had to go on stage in my robot costume and dance alongside the girls in their sexy, shiny leather outfits. It felt awkward and I was embarrassed because I felt like I looked ridiculous and out of place. But I had to do it.

Wardrobe immediately saw how bizarre it was. They ended up making me my very own gold corset with gold leggings. They also didn't have shoes for me. For the first leg of the tour, I wore my own heels – the same heels I wore in rehearsals (after replacing the pair that broke). After all, I was only supposed to be a mannequin. But I'd danced my way to being more than a mannequin.

In spite of the intensity during production rehearsals, I was enjoying every moment of the experience. This was going to be my first world tour! Nothing could shake that joy! Prior to this tour, the only country I had been to outside of the U.S. was Japan.

We were getting ready to kick off the tour in Canada, but we still didn't know who was going to be performing "Single Ladies" with Beyoncé and Ashley Everett. Out of all the numbers in the show, I really wanted to do "Single Ladies." And to my astonishment, I was chosen.

Me? The same girl who butchered this routine during the callback auditions and the only non-trained, female dancer on the tour!

But once again, just when I thought the odds were against me, they were for me. I was honored. This was Beyoncé's most popular single and video to date, and it was the closing number for the tour, so every single one of her fans was going to be anticipating the live performance of "Single Ladies."

And now that they trusted me to do that number, I wasn't going to let Beyoncé, Frank, JaQuel, or myself down.

As we took off to Canada for the debut show of the *I Am...*World Tour, I flashed back to the short timeline of events that had taken place professionally up to this moment. Just a year ago, I'd begun my first national tour as a back-up dancer for The Dream. Exactly one year later, I was beginning my first WORLD tour as a back-up dancer for Beyoncé. And within that year was the start of my working relationship with the inspiration behind my dream – Jamaica Craft and Ciara.

I wasn't sure why I was chosen to embark on this path, but I did know that people had come into my life who believed in me and were pushing me to extend further than I'd gone thus far. I felt blessed beyond measure.

March 26, 2008, it was show time. A new wave of inspiration was emerging. A new journey had begun. There I was – at the foundation of a new dream.

Lessons From I Am...
Part 1: The Process

- Divine intervention is real. Growing up in church, I learned that faith requires trust when the course of life changes. Now it was time to apply what I'd learned.

- When your life is on a new journey, expect the unexpected. But believe, without any doubt, that the course you're taking is routing you to a great destination.

- This was the beginning of an evolution from the dream I started with. I saw my dream realized prior to embarking on The *I Am…*World Tour, and now I was entering a new world of inspiration and dreams.

- There are a lot of components that go into a world tour production. This was a process I'd never seen before – and it was the start of a new dynamic of work ethic for me and understanding the importance of a strong team.

Chapter Four

I Am...Part 2: My Crowning Glory

*"I am not my hair; I am not this skin
I am not your expectations no
I am not my hair; I am not this skin
I am a soul that lives within."*

—India. Arie

EVER HEARD THE EXPRESSION that hair is a woman's crowning glory? Hair *is* a BIG deal, especially in the African-American community. You can go to any black hair salon and find women under the dryers, in the stylist's chairs, and in the waiting area. Every single day of the week. Whether it's for a relaxer, a press and curl, a weave, a shampoo set, or styling a natural "do," we are there and ready to spend a pretty penny. It's just as big of a deal in the dance industry. Hair can make or break you booking a gig. Seriously.

I've received all of the above mentioned styles since my first visit to a hair salon. I was nine years old when I got my first relaxer and continued to do so until I decided to go natural at nineteen. I loved getting a relaxer, but as a dancer, it got pretty annoying sweating out my perm every week. I usually waited at least four weeks before my next relaxer. I always had a thick head of hair, so when my new growth kicked in, it was something serious.

The majority of the time I was in college, I wore a flat twist style in the front of my hair and had it flat ironed in the back. It seemed like practically the entire campus at Bennett College had natural hair –braided styles and healthy and neat Afros. It was beautiful. Three of my good friends from Couture Productions rocked gorgeous locs. I was inspired to go natural being around so many people who didn't have a relaxer, yet their hair looked healthy and as fresh as it wanted to be.

When I moved back home to Atlanta in September of 2005, I decided I was going to grow my relaxer out. This was difficult for me because I didn't have the patience to deal with half of my head having thick, coarse new growth, and the other portion of my hair being straight and easier to maintain.

So in April of 2006, I decided to do the BC – Big Chop. It looks exactly how it sounds. I cut all my hair OFF and got it dyed a slightly lighter shade than my naturally dark, brown hair.

I was officially rocking a TWA, teeny weeny Afro. It was different for me. I had never seen my face without hair around it, but I liked it. I started going to auditions with my hair short, but as my hair started growing back, I didn't know what in the world to do with it. I didn't have patience to try different natural styles to see what would work for me. I was ready for a weave.

In the dance community, it's not only about your talent, it's about your look. Back in 2006, I wasn't feeling my TWA look as a dancer. I always loved big, curly hair, so I tried the Tracee Ellis Ross look. But I have such a small head, that look wasn't it for me. Plus, I was used to dealing with thick but straight hair all my life. I had no idea how to properly maintain thick, curly hair.

Next, I did a long, wavy style with bangs. This look was cute on me. It didn't swallow my head, and I thought the bangs helped bring attention to the shape of my eyes. But boy, if I didn't look like every other dancer in Atlanta! There was no way I was standing out with that hairstyle. And if they're looking for just one dancer with long hair and bangs, it's going to be me against the entire room.

Thereafter, I tried a few other styles – long, bone straight, bohemian style and even the Indian, wavy hair. But nothing stuck with me. And when I unbraided my hair after rocking a weave for an extended period of time, I had a HUGE and extremely thick Afro. I was overwhelmed and ready to give in to the idea of getting a relaxer again. I was curious to see how long my hair was after cutting it all off almost two years before.

In December 2007, I was back to wearing a relaxer, but this time, I had shorter hair. I loved how I looked with short, straight hair. But there was NO way I was going to be able to dance with my hair relaxed. So I was back to covering up my hair, but this time, I was wearing clip-on wigs. Since my hair was straight in the front, I was able to blend my hair with the wig. And that's exactly how my hair was for my first tour as a professional dancer. I danced for The Dream in spring of 2008 with a wig on my head.

By summer of 2008, I was ready to rock my short hairstyle, but incorporated some hairpieces to make it easier to maintain. I wanted to have some fun, blonde pieces in my hair without having to dye my natural hair. Thus, the asymmetrical short hairstyle became my defining look, as I danced alongside Ciara in the "Stepped on my J's" video and 2008 BET Awards. It was also my look as I did promotional shows with Jamaican pop artist, Tami Chynn. I felt I had found my individual style. Then, in December of 2008, my hair as I knew it took a turn for the worst. Or rather, the best!

It was my first time getting my hair bonded, and I got it done per recommendation of my then stylist. According to her, it would give my hair more room to flow freely as opposed to looking so "placed" while I danced. I was hesitant at first, and I should've gone with my gut. But instead, I said, "Sure, let's try it."

I absolutely did NOT like it.

Those bonding pieces kept breaking off every time I combed them, and it made my weave get thinner and thinner. I was completely over it and ready to take the bonding style out of my head.

I was so upset at the stylist for suggesting something that ended up not working, that I went back the stylist who had given me my first relaxer since I went natural. But to my dismay, he wasn't experienced with taking out bonded hair. By the end of that salon visit, I was left with uneven, thin, short hair. I was livid. There was no way I could do anything with my hair looking so damaged.

Guess it was back to the TWA. But this time, I had them cut my hair COMPLETELY OFF. Like a Caesar cut. I wanted to strip my hair of EVERYTHING and start over.

It was emotionally and spiritually significant for me because so much had happened so suddenly, and I felt like I was getting ready to transition into a new chapter or phase of my life, but wasn't completely sure what it was.

I just knew it was *something*. That something turned out to be Beyoncé's *I Am…* World Tour.

Even though I'd cut my hair off, I still danced with a wig as I privately let my hair grow out. My initial feeling was that no one was going to see my head until I had some hair back on it. A few weeks after the chop, I only had a TWA. I didn't process it as a new look for me professionally, so I was still planning on dancing with a wig or a weave.

On the day of the *I Am...* tour auditions, I was wearing an asymmetrical wig for the *106&Park* performance with Keri Hilson because that had been my look prior to me cutting my hair off.

To my surprise, after the audition, Beyoncé asked, "What is your hair like underneath that wig?"

Uh oh…

I told her, "It's a very, very short Afro."

She wanted to see a picture of it. I was mortified. Although I'd cut my hair in the past, and at times wore it naturally for go-go jobs, my hair hadn't been *this* short, so even I was still getting used to it. But after seeing my natural hair when we were shooting some video content for the tour, Beyoncé said directly to me, "That's it. That's going to be your look for tour."

What? What do you mean boss lady? I'm going to be the only dancer on stage with no hair? Oh my goodness, this can't be happening.

Maybe I should've been excited because it was unique, but I wasn't thinking like that at the time. I was scared out of my mind. I'd NEVER danced in front of THOUSANDS of people without a weave or a wig on my head. But I had to remember that faith requires trust when the courses change.

To my amazement, there was a second part to it. Not only was I going to be wearing my teeny weeny Afro, it was going to get dyed blonde. Me? A blonde? I didn't see it.

But it all starts with a vision. Beyoncé saw the vision and that was a huge inspiration to me. I knew what it was like to visualize, but she was taking me to another playing field with it.

A short, blonde Afro turned out to be my defining look as a professional dancer.

At first though, I was still set on convincing Beyoncé that I could rock a long weave dancing with her. I went to a wig store in Brooklyn before rehearsal one day, and bought a curly wig that I wore to the rehearsal the following afternoon. It phased her none. Clearly, because on opening night in Edmonton, Canada, I was rocking my teeny, weeny dark Afro, dancing boldly in front of thousands of screaming fans.

Less than one month after opening night of the *I Am…*World Tour, I was on set to shoot my first music video with Beyoncé for her new single, "Sweet Dreams." I was pleasantly surprised to be shooting this video because I wasn't in the routine for tour. I felt honored to be selected to dance with Beyoncé for the music video.

When it came to the hair for the shoot, it would be my first experience trying on a lace wig. But the amount of hair was so dramatic for my small face, I ended up rocking my natural hair. It would be my first feature in a music video without a wig or weave. What a liberating feeling.

My hair wasn't quite blonde yet because I hadn't gone to a stylist to dye it, out of anxiety about how it could turn out. My faith in hair stylists was severely tarnished at this point.

When did the blonde come in? I'll never forget the day.

It was May 18, 2009. We were in Lisbon, Portugal, and it was a show day. Bright and early in the morning, I made my way to Beyoncé's hair stylist's room and it was there, the morning of our show in Portugal, that her stylist, Neal Farinah, applied bleach on my hair for the first time ever. In my life.

Do you understand how nervous I was? I kept it cool on the outside, but on the inside, I was freaking out. However my hair turned out that day was exactly how I would have to rock it, on stage, in front of thousands of people, that very night. There was no wig store I could run to and cover my hair up if it turned out to be a disaster. In that very moment, on that very day, my crowning glory lay in the hands of Neal Farinah.

It turned out strikingly beautiful. When I looked in the mirror for the first time after he bleached my hair, I was completely shocked. It was no turning back for me. I was the girl with the platinum blonde hair.

It took some getting used to the first few times I did make-up with the blonde hair because I didn't have to go as dramatic as I did with dark hair. My hair was serving all the drama I needed.

After he applied the bleach to my hair, it was going to be my responsibility to maintain it. How in the world was I going to do that? For the next four months, every time I needed a touch-up, it was a gamble because I was going to a different hair salon on the road to get my hair re-bleached.

It took me a long time to get comfortable knowing when it was okay to bleach my hair again. I didn't want to get it done too soon, but I swear, only a week after getting a retouch, I had dirty blonde hair all over again.

Finally, I decided to trust myself, and touch up my own hair. Neal provided me with the ingredients to color my hair platinum blonde. Can you believe I tried to bleach my hair for the first time, the day BEFORE the DVD shooting of the tour? For some reason, I like living on the edge. Now, my crowning glory lay in MY hands. Thank God, it turned out great.

It took me not only wearing a short, blonde Afro on stage dancing behind the world's biggest female artist of this generation, it took me OWNING it. Ever since that pivotal day on May 18, 2009, I haven't looked back. When I walked on that stage in Lisbon, Portugal, this surge of confidence and knowingness took over me. I felt like I was proclaiming, "Here I am!"

It felt indescribably freeing. I was coming into my own woman and what better person to introduce that to me than the world's biggest, female megastar. I was learning far more from my career as a dancer than I could ever imagine. I was learning how every person on the team plays an important part in the success of a production, so our best self should always be represented, and that included me on this tour.

I discovered the answer to my question from tour rehearsals. "Where do I fit in?" Well, I fit in, to stand out. We all did. There was no world tour production going on that had the combination of dancers that Beyoncé had.

It's liberating walking around with nothing to hide behind. Female dancers can get caught up in performing with hair because it makes dance movement look more powerful, extreme and dramatic. But what if you can do that without hair? That's what I realized. Just because I was the only one on stage without big or long hair didn't mean I was going to get lost on stage.

I didn't even realize how inspiring it would be for women of color around the world and women who were aspiring dancers and even professional dancers to go for a natural and short, blonde look. It's an honor to be a person of inspiration in that realm because the look changed my own life. My hair is indeed my crowning glory.

Lessons From I Am: Part 2: My Crowning Glory

- This experience was that new chapter and spiritual transformation I believed I was approaching when I cut off all my hair a few months prior to tour. It was no coincidence that my hair sparked an intuitive notion of change.

- Inspiration is contagious in the entertainment industry and people like to see something familiar, but unique. That's why the best celebrity style and fashion can create a chain of inspiration for years to come.

- Hair is a huge contributing factor to working as a female dancer in this industry. In the entertainment industry, it's not only about your talent, it's also about your look. Back in 2006, when I did my first hair Big Chop – BC, I wasn't feeling my Teeny weeny afro as a dancer. Three years later, it became my signature. Your look is very important. If you can rock a sexy, unique hairstyle, go for it. There's nothing wrong with being courageous and standing out.

- Dare to be different. It could change your life.

Chapter Five

I Am...Part 3:

The World Tour

Being on a world tour is a magical, fast-paced experience. There's exposure to a lot of cities in a short amount of time, and with this being my first world tour, I would come to understand concert pandemonium in a major way.

The crowds overseas were completely different from the crowds in the States. International crowds had no problem screaming at the top of their lungs from the opening number to the closing number and for everything in between.

On the first leg of the *I Am…* World Tour, we went to Canada. Cold weather and beautiful cities. Here, we made the necessary tweaks to the show to make sure before we went to Europe next, the overall production was solid.

We went to Europe for two separate legs. One leg, we were there for a month and a half and the other, for two weeks. I had my first experiences teaching dance classes in cities from Manchester, UK to Dublin, Ireland. It blew my mind that I was in a dance studio in another country, teaching hip-hop to another culture of people.

How did my life get here?

Traveling the world was opening me up in ways I never thought. But when you're on tour with the most popular, female entertainer in the world, people are enthusiastic to be around her team as well. For us dancers, that meant people learning dance steps from us and taking lots of photos wherever we walked.

To be identified on the street took me by surprise. I'm just doing what I love, and hadn't processed how visible we were to the world because of video and photo content from the tour. But then I remembered, as a fan of artists, I absolutely know who their dancers and their musicians are. Here I am, working for someone who has massive global appeal, and I was sporting a very unique look, so there was no escaping being recognized.

The U.S. leg of the tour came third. This would be the first time my mom, my agent, my dad, and a few of my friends would see me perform live in a concert. My mom and agent came to the Atlanta show while my Dad came to the Philadelphia show.

We were in Philadelphia when Michael Jackson unexpectedly passed away on June 25, 2009. Michael Jackson is one of a dancer's greatest inspirations, so we were all devastated and heartbroken. What made the memory worse was that the assistant choreographer for the *I Am…World Tour*, Chris Grant, was in rehearsals to go on tour as a back-up dancer for Michael. We couldn't imagine how devastating that was for him to be in the middle of living out his dream, and it come to a tragic halt.

Our performance in Philadelphia was the night following Michael's passing. "Halo" was the closing song of the concert, and before "Halo" started, Michael's picture went on display on the projection screen and the entire arena erupted in screams. It would be a tribute Beyoncé kept in the show every night for the remainder of the tour.

Shortly after that, a few of the dancers were flown to Los Angeles to perform at the 2009 *BET Awards* with Beyoncé. I was one of the dancers. I couldn't believe I was back at the *BET Awards* for the second year in a row, and this time with Beyoncé. Although we didn't play a big role in the performance – she sang *"Ave Maria"* with a visual tribute to Michael Jackson – I was honored to be there and happy to see Chris Grant who was assisting.

Before the start of our leg in Australia in the fall of 2009, Beyoncé was slated to perform "Single Ladies" at the *MTV Video Music Awards* in New York. The performance would include a cast of fifty female dancers. This performance reunited me with dancers I had previously worked with on Ciara and The Dream, and also dancers I was meeting for the first time. It was an incredible experience to share the stage with so many women and work with familiar and new talent.

Immediately after the performance, I was on a private jet to Australia.

Besides, Brazil and Dublin, Australia takes the crown for the best audience of the *I Am…*World Tour. They made me feel that magical energy that was familiar from performing in Madison Square Garden.

On October 13, 2009, we had a show on my birthday. We were in Osaka, Japan and at the end of the show, Beyoncé turned around and sang "Happy Birthday" to me. It was a beautiful and touching surprise.

So much had taken place in my life. To be out of the country dancing back-up with an icon on my birthday was unforgettable. My tour mates gave me one of the most memorable birthdays I'd ever had. From a karaoke party, to dancing the night away, and then receiving a gift from the boss herself, my life had become something I'd never dreamed of.

What inspired me the most was seeing how much a person's light could brighten so many people's lives around the world. Not only was Beyoncé impacting the individuals she hired to be a part of her team, she was impacting the world with her talent and energy. I felt inspired to make my visions bigger than ever before.

So many moments on the tour had me wide-eyed, in awe and amazement of my life as a dancer and of the world – from climbing the Great Wall of China after flying into Beijing, jumping off yachts after dance rehearsals in Abu Dhabi, and performing on an award show in Berlin, Germany. Watching the Eiffel Tower twinkle in the sky at midnight in Paris, visiting the Schonbrunn Palace in Vienna, taking a boat tour of the city of Stockholm, walking around famous temples and chapels, or visiting the biggest castle in the world in Prague, Czech Republic was how I spent days off the stage.

As winter of 2009 approached, we were coming to the final shows scheduled on the *I Am…World Tour*. As far as personnel knew, the tour was ending after our last show in Europe on November 24, 2009.

While back at home from the tour, I had reconnected with Jamaica Craft who I hadn't seen or spoken to since I'd performed on *106&Park* nine months ago.

She had reached out to me about an inquiry that spoke to my quest for a bigger vision. Jamaica was putting together a girl group and wanted me to join. She'd heard from a dancer who I'd gone to high school with that I could sing. When she asked if I was interested, there was no hesitation on my end.

I was astonished at how God was ordering my steps, and aligning people and circumstances to change my life and expand my dreams.

I was preparing to sing in a girl group that would be spearheaded by the very woman who created the movement in a music video that had inspired my journey. It was perfect to me.

Here I was, on tour with a woman who came from a massively successful girl group, and had evolved into a solo megastar. Seeing her share not just one of her gifts, but multiple, showed me how life-changing that can be. I wanted to change lives just like the people God had placed on my path changed mine.

Shortly before Christmas 2009, I got word that one more leg had been added to the tour and we would be going to Brazil in February, with a final stop in Trinidad and Tobago.

While on break from the tour, I got directly booked on a music video by Usher's veteran choreographer –

Aakomon "AJ" Jones. I was recommended to him by Amy Allen, one of Jamaica Craft's assistant choreographers, who also assisted Aakomon. He wanted to hire me to dance in Usher's new music video, "Hey Daddy (Daddy's Home)."

This would be my first time dancing in a music video with my short, blonde hair. Since I'd been on tour with Beyoncé, I hadn't worked with any other artists. So to now be able to add a music legend like Usher to my resume before this magical year ended, had me on a cloud.

Ciara. Beyoncé. Now Usher. What was next for my journey?

After 108 successful shows, on February 18, 2010, the *I Am…World Tour* came to end.

I was just starting out professionally in Atlanta only a year ago, and two years later, I'd seen every continent but Africa and Antarctica.

The number of fans I acquired from all over the world showed me how powerful entertainment is. From my love of dancing, I was fortunate enough to perform on stages around the globe and touch the hearts of people by sharing my gift. Going on a world tour gave me an outpour of love from people in places I'd never imagine I'd make friends in. From Turkey to Brazil to Japan and England, I saw my network of friends increase. From dancing.

Now it was time to take everything I had learned on this tremendous journey and apply it to my new journey in a singing group.

Lessons from I Am: Part 3: The World Tour

- The world we live in is so magnificent, and filled with a diversity of beautiful people and energy. It is a privilege to see the world at large and humbling to explore various cultures and countries. Reality sets in that the world is so much bigger than us.

- Dreams are meant to evolve as we evolve. Go with the flow.

- I remember going to Japan for the first time in the summer of 2008. And I said, "Lord, if I can go to Europe next year that would be great. Anywhere in Europe. Like, London. I would be so happy." I didn't even set my mind on going a world tour! I was just looking at going to one place in Europe. God gave me the whole world! Dream BIG. The more impossible it seems, the better, because anything is truly possible in this world.

Chapter Six

OMG

"The turning point in the process of growing up is when you discover the core of strength within you that survives all hurt."

—Max Lerner

HERE IT WAS, Spring 2010. Following Beyoncé's, *I Am...*World Tour, the momentum was strong in my dance career, and I was now experiencing more direct bookings – working jobs without auditioning.

I booked a second music video with Usher, this time for his new single with Will.I.Am, "OMG." For the opening dance sequence of the video, I was placed on the front line. The pressure was on.

To have a technically trained choreographer like Amy Allen trust me with her movement and an artist of Usher's caliber trust me with an opening visual in his video, spoke volumes and was not something I took lightly. I was still new on the dance scene, and felt I had a lot to show and prove, not just to myself, but to the choreographers and artists that I was hired to work with. As unpredictable as my life was, I knew every job was fuel to my growth along this journey.

After shooting "OMG," the director from the video, Anthony Mandler, booked me on another music video he was directing for rapper Drake, and his new single, "Over." It was my first time shooting a solo scene in a music video, and as nervous as I initially was because the experience was so new for me, I transformed those nerves into adrenaline and let myself be fully present in the moment.

I was also giving my musical background a chance to flourish, and began artist development with my new singing group put together by Jamaica Craft. Spending the summer working with Jamaica in both music and dance was a significant reality of a dream.

I was working with The Dream, the first artist I had started with two years prior, for his new album, *Love King*. I was also back on the road dancing with Ciara as she was promoting her new album, *Basic Instinct*. I was simultaneously having recording sessions, dance rehearsals, personal training sessions, and stage performance rehearsals with the group, so there was a beautiful chain of events taking place.

The first dance job I ever turned down was for promotional shows overseas with Usher. He was promoting his new album, *Raymond v. Raymond* and as much as I wanted to do the job, I was the maid of honor in my best friend's wedding, and the show dates were around the same time. I just knew I wouldn't get called to work for Usher again, because who turns down a job for him?

It wouldn't be my last opportunity to work with Usher after all.

On September 23, 2010, once again, I was presented with an opportunity I hadn't expected – to be a back-up dancer on Usher's *OMG* tour. As a dancer, there was no question about wanting to work with Usher. Besides the fact that he represented the A-town, I was a true fan of his music. On top of that, I always loved the choreography he did because it was saucy, clean, and always provided just the right dose of ATL-inspired flavor. But I never anticipated touring with Usher.

There was buzz that he was looking for dancers for his upcoming tour, but I was completely dedicated to and focused on the singing group I was in. I was prepared to say no to any auditions or direct books to be on this tour. And I did just that. Twice.

I said no to the artistic director of the tour, Barry Lather, whom I have great respect for. When asked by my agent if I would go on tour with Usher, I again said no. But by the third time being asked to join the tour, I felt it was time to really go into my prayer closet and talk to God.

I literally asked God, "Why? Why is it that I am being offered this opportunity three times? There's a plethora of female dancers that auditioned for this gig that upon first offer would've said yes. So why is this being practically given to me?" Here I was starting a new journey with my singing group and now I was being offered to go on one of the biggest tours of the year as a dancer.

I felt I had come to the point where I had done all that I wanted to do as a dancer and it was time to move on. But maybe I wasn't done doing all that I *needed* to do as a dancer. I was so eager to start a new journey. I didn't realize I hadn't finished trekking this one.

At a real crossroads in my journey, my decision would be the hardest I'd made. But with it, growth would come.

After a long talk with Jamaica, a long talk with my Dad, and another long talk with God, I made the decision to accept the offer to go on Usher's 2010-11 *OMG* Tour.

The next morning, I had my suitcases packed and was on a flight from Atlanta to Los Angeles to begin a new experience.

Rehearsals for tour were unlike any process I was previously familiar with. There were six choreographers that we had to work with, so there were a variety of styles to learn and constant changes. The choreography for tour was on an intricate level I hadn't been introduced to before. I was working with a new vocabulary of dancing and experiencing true, on-the-job training.

I was also dancing alongside an elite squad of talent I was working with for the first time, and a large majority of the dancers had years of previous touring experience. But one of the familiar faces was a fellow dancer from the *I Am…*World Tour – Ashley Seldon.

Rehearsals for tour were split between two dance studios in Hollywood, California. One studio, International Dance Academy, was in a central tourist hub on Hollywood Boulevard. The other studio, Alley Kat, was a more low-key rehearsal space, but a popular location for iconic music entertainers. These two studios were where I learned classic Usher choreography like, "Caught Up," "U Don't Have to Call," and "Yeah."

We usually worked no less than twelve hour days, and strength and conditioning workouts were the norm prior to start of rehearsals. We were also given printed handouts of the stage so that we could mark our spacing for every number we danced in. This was the behind-the-scenes process that I never imagined tour rehearsals for Usher entailed. It was so necessary, however, to build and maintain stamina and endurance long-term and to increase spatial awareness, which is so crucial for dancers.

While in tour rehearsals, Usher continued his promotions for the new album *Raymond v. Raymond*, so we all flew to Germany and London to perform on the singing competition show, *X-Factor*. Just a year prior, I spent my birthday in Japan for Beyoncé's tour. This time, I spent it flying from London to Los Angeles for Usher's tour rehearsals.

These were moments in my journey that I could not have predicted. I just knew I was grateful to work for and learn from greats, because you can only become better learning from the best.

After six weeks of intense training and rehearsals, the *OMG* tour kicked off on November 10, 2010 in Seattle, Washington.

While Beyoncé and her team were more hands on with the look of each dancer for tour, Usher's team was more open to let the female dancers decide how we wanted our hair to be. Makeovers are always exciting, and I had been rocking my hair short and blonde for a year and half by now, so although it became my identity on the *I Am…*Tour, I thought I could try something different for Usher's tour.

By the fourth show, I was back to my short blonde 'do.

The first leg of the tour was in the U.S. and Canada, and tour was flowing smoothly until we got to Virginia in December, and Usher fell ill and had to cancel the show.

A few days later, a blog came out about Usher and his cancelled show, and my name and social media pictures were included in it. We were in New York City at Madison Square Garden on December 13, 2010 for the first of two shows there.

This particular morning came with an unusual number of messages on my phone from family and friends. They were all contacting me about a blog from *MediaTakeOut*™ that insinuated that Usher and I had been sleeping together and his girlfriend finding out was the reason the Virginia show was cancelled! It was a bizarre story that I couldn't believe I was at the center of.

But I didn't panic. I called his then girlfriend and gave her the heads-up about the article. I knew none of it was true, so out of confidence and respect, I contacted her first to make sure she was aware. Of course it made for juicy gossip, but I couldn't understand why I would be the target of false information.

I realized by dancing in two of Usher's recent music videos and then being selected to go on tour with him, it looked like there could be something going on between us. Not to mention a skit in the show to his song, "U Remind Me," where I played his love interest.

I had never experienced anything more awkward than being at the venue that day. Everyone from the band, to the dancers, to the crew were asking me if I was all right. When we did an exclusive sound check for a group of fans, I could feel the energy as we did, "U Remind Me." They just knew the rumors had to be true, and I knew I couldn't change their minds.

From that moment, I promised myself that I wouldn't waver in my performance quality with Usher because of what it may look like to people. I would be unrelenting. Dancing for a male artist as a female is way more intimate and hands-on than it is dancing for a female artist.

While female artists feed off of the energy of their female dancers, male artists feed off of the energy and chemistry with their female dancers. These were the kinds of things I wouldn't understand unless I experienced them. Why I was learning it in this way was unbeknownst to me, but what I did know was that God makes *no* mistakes and this was all a part of my growth and strengthening my character.

As undeniably attractive as Usher is, I had no interest in sleeping with the boss. My only interest was doing the best job I could possibly do as a dancer and performer. Besides, I had someone special in my life.

After a while, the hype around the blog simmered down, and there were only a few weeks left before the end of the first leg and the start of a new year.

New Year's Eve 2010 was an unforgettable celebration! It was the first time I would bring in the New Year at an arena, performing on stage, and in front of thousands of people. We had just finished performing, "Hey Daddy" and here we were on stage, in Miami, Florida being handed glasses of champagne. We watched the countdown to 2011 on the projection screen, and to top it off, I had my favorite cousin in the world, Malishas, on stage right next to me! It was truly perfect! I was doing what I love, entering into a new year, and I had my family with me! It was a great time.

We didn't stop moving after New Year's. In fact, the pace picked up even more. We were back in rehearsals literally two days later to prepare for the European leg of the tour.

The first show of the European leg was in Berlin, Germany on January 12, 2011. Never had my heart broken for someone I worked for like it did for Usher this night. Prior to the show, it was vaguely evident that Usher wasn't feeling well, but being the professional, hard-worker he is, he didn't want to cancel his show and decided to perform under the weather.

Halfway through the show, Usher looked like he was in pain. While in the middle of singing, "There Goes My

Baby," he stopped the music, apologized to his fans, and walked off stage. The rest of the show was cancelled.

I know it was disappointing for his fans as much as it was confusing, but then you realize and understand that entertainers are human. They're not robots or machines, and they go through real situations just like anyone else. Tour schedules are extremely intense and leave little to no room for downtime. If there are personal matters going on, they get crammed in with the busy day-to-day demands of touring. Usher's fans that night just happened to witness an honest person at a breaking point.

Less than a week later, Usher had fully recovered and the tour commenced in Lyon, France.

February 2011 was, hands down, the most action-packed month of the tour. We kicked off the month performing two shows in London, England and then flew back to the U.S. to perform at the *Superbowl XLV Halftime Show*. This was my first Superbowl performance and it was a moment like nothing I'd ever taken in before. Hundreds of thousands of screaming fans and the massive capacity of a stadium field was a jaw-dropping sight to see for the first time. Here I was on national television performing for the highest rated sporting event, watched by millions!

How far I'd come in just three years was more than I could've imagined.

Next, we performed at the Grammy's. Rehearsals for Grammy's 2011 was one of my all-time favorite moments in my career thus far. I always loved the choreography for the "OMG" breakdown, and choreographer, Aakomon Jones, threw down in the formations and choreography he created for the Grammy performance, so as a dancer and performer, I enjoyed not only working with him, but also the elite squad of dancers I got to perform with.

Immediately following the Grammys, it was Valentine's Day and we were flying to the city of love itself – Paris.

As soon as we landed, we hit the stage. A week after Paris, we were back in London for another two shows, and shooting the *OMG* Tour DVD.

Our heads were spinning and our bodies aching, but it was so much fun. We were performing in all of my favorite international cities from London to Amsterdam to Dublin, so I was able to revisit restaurants, places, people, and even clubs that I enjoyed from touring with Beyoncé. There were also new places I was visiting – Dubai, U.A.E., Shanghai, China, and Auckland, New Zealand.

It truly was a whirlwind of experiences and emotions, but the best of times because as rapidly as events were taking place, so were my personal and professional growth. A lot of hard work and sleepless nights accommodated this tour, but it was all gratifying.

The tour had come into a really nice groove since it first began in November, and alas in April, after completing shows in Europe followed by Asia, and then Australia, we had our first extended break since we started tour rehearsals seven months prior. It was much needed time off, but there was also the bittersweet realization that we were approaching the end of tour.

For the final leg, we returned to the U.S., and on June 1, 2011 we performed the last show for the *OMG* Tour. We ended it at the Staples Center in Los Angeles, CA, the city I would call home two months later.

All in all, the *OMG* experience came with some tough moments to get through, but there were equally joyful moments cherished. I felt my growth as a dancer. I felt my newfound confidence as a woman, my knowingness from experience, my strengthened faith, and my mental maturity.

It was the most well-rounded experience of my dance career and I am so grateful for every moment that made me say, "Oh my gosh!" The tour's title was very befitting of the adventures.

Lessons From OMG

- Embrace change. It always precedes growth.
- Entertainers are human. Entertainers are real. They are expected to be perfect, but seeing them otherwise is honest and admirable.
- Every team has a different regimen to ensure the success of what they are undertaking, but the common theme of successful teams is hard work and dedication.
- People might make up false stories and make you the target, but don't allow bad intentions to ruin a good heart.

Chapter Seven

Mrs. Marvelous

"So they are no longer two, but one flesh. Therefore what God has joined together, let no one separate."

—Matthew 19:6

I KNEW IT. I could feel God pulling me on this journey, whispering to me to pay attention. The Universe was moving forcefully. I've never been in a tornado, but the imagery comes to mind when I think about the way God brought my husband and I together. It felt like there was so much noise, so much distraction presenting itself externally, that it cautioned me to tune in to my spirit. Once I did, and then I looked at him, everything around me went silent.

Marc and I first met in the summer of 2010 on a gig with Usher to perform "OMG" on *So You Think You Can Dance*. There was a great line-up of dancers for the performance, and Marc was one of the male dancers.

Professionally, he was known as Marvelous, and I recognized him from my research year's prior as being among the top dancers, based out of Brooklyn, New York.

I remember him being exactly that in rehearsals, too. A really incredible dancer that moved in a way I hadn't seen a dancer move before. His movement intrigued me. But we barely exchanged any words on the job. So it was surprising that Marc reached out to me a few weeks later on Facebook.

Blackberry instant messaging was still very popular during this time, so we exchanged info to communicate that way. I didn't think much of it, but we continued to text, and then texts turned into phone calls, and phone calls turned into Skype video calls. A friendship had ensued between us.

At the end of the summer, we ran into each other at Usher's Pre-Grammy party in Los Angeles. He had come with Usher, and I came with Ciara, which was the first time I had gone to a party with her.

By this time, production was underway for Usher's upcoming tour and Marc was one of the two male dancers Usher had been using for his promo run, so it was a no-brainer that Marc would be on the tour.

One night, Marc called me with the heads up that Usher's choreographer would be reaching out to me about the tour. Next thing we knew, we went from seeing each other on Skype every day, to seeing each other in rehearsal every day. Immediately, our budding friendship went into business mode.

We still texted and called each other on our down time. As friends. But we were starting to like each other.

For the partner section of a song we performed for tour called "Hot Tottie" and "Love in This Club," Marc and I were dance partners. We were both inexperienced in partner dancing, but it was fun working together and building the necessary trust to pull partnering off successfully. The partner section for "Hot Tottie" eventually got scrapped, but there was something steadily brewing between the two of us.

As much as we tried to keep it private during tour, and not put too much pressure on what was developing, the chemistry was undeniable.

We spent the Christmas holiday together in Atlanta after discovering both our parents resided there, and by the time we were on the European leg of the tour in early 2011, we were saying, "I love you."

When we had a few weeks break from tour in April, we travelled to Barbados together for vacation and he introduced me to his family there. Besides performing in Trinidad and Tobago during the *I Am…*tour, this was my first time going to an island, and I was mesmerized by the atmosphere. To be around family on an island was such a peaceful and warm experience. With the fast pace of tour life, it was a breath of fresh air to be still and share that moment with someone I loved.

For Easter, we attended church together. That was huge for me because although I'd grown up in church, my attendance had waned since graduating high school. I continued my spiritual journey outside of church, and although my faith in God and belief in Christ was prevalent, I had no church home.

Events were taking place so quickly in my life. I didn't even realize that I missed that fellowship with like believers.

Up to this point, I hadn't attended church with anyone I had been significantly involved with. I felt with Marc, we were grounding each other in a way I hadn't known before as we continued the grind in our careers. As hurried as our lives were, time together seemed to balance the pace out, because we would simply slow down with each other.

As soon as tour ended in June, we took a cruise to the Bahamas to celebrate Marc's birthday and the end of a long and successful tour.

By the end of summer of 2011, I packed up my belongings and my puppy, and moved to Los Angeles.

In a matter of a year, our relationship had become very serious. As exciting and brand new as it all was, we didn't want to get caught up in the fantasy world that tour life can project. But after tour was over, we still wanted to be together. There was something that felt right about us.

A few years later, I realized that the *OMG* tour was also a journey to my husband. Okay, I know I started this chapter off with I knew it, but I had NO clue! I knew God wanted me to pay attention, but I thought it was just career-oriented. I didn't know I was developing a relationship with the man who would become my husband.

We were blessed to travel the world together as we were building a relationship for the long-term.

For the next year and a half following the *OMG* tour, Marc and I continued to work together dancing for Usher. By tour's end, word had spread around the camp that Marc and I were an item, so we no longer had to hide it. And if you let them tell the story, some would say they already knew or they saw it coming all along!

In March 2012, I travelled to the continent of Africa for the first time. Marc and I had a show with Usher in Johannesburg, South Africa, and it was the most incredible trip. Nothing could describe how blessed I felt being in Africa, dancing for an icon, and sharing the experience alongside my significant other.

I had never gone on a hot air balloon ride, and it was unforgettable to do it for the first time in Johannesburg, with Marc right by my side as took in a panoramic view of the entire city. We went on safaris together, Segway rides through an African zoo, and enjoyed meeting and dancing with native Africans.

The last professional job Marc and I did together was in January 2013 for the Presidential Inauguration Concert in Washington, D.C. To perform in the presence of President Obama and First Lady Michelle Obama was a moment I'd never forget. This was history at its finest.

To be a part of a celebratory event such as the second inauguration of our first black president was truly special. To watch – in person – President Obama and Michelle Obama slow dance together was as moving as it was captivating. The Commander-in-Chief and First Lady were displaying in a most genuine way how beautiful, powerful, and substantial love between two people is.

In that moment, I was grateful to know I had a love of my own.

Working with someone who was just as involved in the industry as I was made it easy for us to understand the demands of our schedules, as well as our need for creative space, and also desire for balance between work and play. As our relationship blossomed through working together, we continued to grow and strengthen our relationship even while working separately. Nothing is more beautiful than a partnership of understanding and respect.

When 2014 rang in, we were basking in all the fresh energy that comes with the arrival of a new year. As a couple, we discussed short and long-term goals for the year ahead, and two major topics came into play. Us living separately and me moving back to Atlanta.

I had lived in Los Angeles for almost three years now, and had gotten hired for some new experiences in my career such as dancing on national television commercials and films. I was also being flown to cities in Brazil and Japan to teach dance workshops, and had even started taking acting classes. But I had an incessant desire to explore my journey in music again.

I hadn't found reliable producers to create with in Los Angeles and was starting to believe that I needed to be back in Atlanta to make music. I was connected with Atlanta-based producers that I could start working with in the studio.

Marc, being the understanding and supportive partner that he was, encouraged me to do what I felt was best for me creatively. Although he wasn't happy with the idea of us being in separate cities, he was happy to see me pursue another passion of mine.

By then, we had both become heavily involved in our church home, Spirit Food Christian Center. It was important to us to establish ourselves in a solid, spiritual community as we continued our respective journeys in our careers. Even though a long-distance relationship isn't the easiest, nor the most ideal situation, we were inspired to treat our relationship honorably, and stop living together before marriage.

However, before I could take flight to Atlanta on March 20, 2014, I would go from being a girlfriend to being a wife.

It was March 18, 2014 and Marc and I were at Tuesday night Bible study. After service, I went up to our pastor – affectionately called Pastor Z – to let him know I wouldn't be at the church for a while and said good-bye for now.

Pastor Z looked at Marc and I with a perplexed expression as I explained to him how I was moving back to Atlanta to begin my new venture in music. He asked if Marc was coming with me. I shook my head, as we explained our decision to live separately until marriage.

He proceeded to ask what was preventing us from getting married in the first place. Here is where it all took a turn.

Marc explained to Pastor Z that, of course, he wanted to propose to me, but he was preparing for the perfect time.

Pastor Z wasn't having it.

He said, "Where in the Bible does it say, 'he who finds a fiancée finds a good thing'? Nowhere. Scripture says, he who finds a *wife* finds a good thing and obtains favor of the Lord."

Marc and I looked at each other in agreement.

"Do you love each other?" Pastor Z asked us.

We nodded our heads and said yes.

"Do you want to spend the rest of your lives together?"

Again we both said yes.

"Then here's what you do. Go down to the County Clerk office in Norwalk and get a marriage license."

Marc and I were mystified. We appreciated him sharing the information, but was he implying that we should do this tomorrow?

I said, "Pastor, I leave on Thursday."

"Great! Call me when you two get the license."

Marc and I couldn't believe what just happened. But our pastor set us all the way straight. Almost four years in, marriage was something we'd discussed as a couple, and knew we wanted. We also knew the only thing that delayed us from being married was the proposal, engagement ring, and of course, the wedding ceremony.

As a woman, I did want these things because I grew up knowing it was a part of the journey to marriage. But our pastor was showing us another way.

Ironically, we were both scheduled to have individual counseling sessions with Pastor Z the following day. My session was first, so I called him and the first thing he asked was, "Did ya'll get the marriage license yet?"

I laughed and said no. This is when I realized our pastor was not playing with us and had the foresight that Marc and I were not to delay becoming man and wife. We were to do it then and there.

"This is not me talking out my neck. This is about obedience and the Holy Spirit's intervention on you and Marc's behalf. Let me talk to Marc."

I don't know what he said to Marc, but after their conversation, we got dressed to head down to the Norwalk county clerk office to get our marriage license. We couldn't believe how suddenly this was taking place. But with both of us strong in faith, we knew it was all right.

After we received our license that afternoon, we called Pastor and let him know the good news. "Pastor we did it. We have our marriage license!"

"Great! I can marry you two at seven thirty tonight in my office! Just bring two witnesses with you and the license."

Marc and I looked at each other like "what"!? We thought we were just getting the license that day and that was it for the time being. We did not expect to get married that evening.

"But Pastor, don't we need rings? We don't have that," I said.

"Don't worry about the rings. The rings will come," is all he said before hanging up.

We only had a few hours before the ceremony, and knew we had to trust God in this journey because things were happening swiftly. Without hesitation, Marc and I knew who we wanted to call to be our witnesses for the ceremony. Derek and Sophia Luke were good spiritual friends of ours who were also a married couple and members of our church. We told them what was going on, and asked if they would be available and willing to attend the ceremony that evening.

Because it was so last minute, we were so relieved that they excitedly agreed to witness. The only question they asked us was what was one of our favorite love songs. They said they would see us that evening.

The events that took place at the ceremony were nothing less than confirmation that God had brought Marc and I together all along.

At seven thirty on the evening of March 19, 2014, Marc and I walked into Pastor Z's chambers to see Derek and Sophia gleaming with excitement. They embraced us and then we sat down to share with them the chain of events that led up to the moment they were getting ready to witness.

The powerful thing about having spiritual friends is that they are tuned in to God in a way that cannot be explained. As believers, we know it's the Holy Spirit. Before the ceremony began, Derek and Sophia shared with us how they had been fasting and consecrating themselves prior to our phone call. Part of their consecration was no communication to the outside world. But when Marc called Derek, something told Derek to answer.

We hadn't told Derek and Sophia about us not having rings, so when Sophia told us that the Holy Spirit told her to go in their drawer and bring the weddings rings that she and Derek had once exchanged when they renewed their vows, I was overcome with emotion. We were given the rings from Derek and Sophia to wear until we were able to exchange rings of our own.

Not only did they provide the rings for Marc and I to exchange our vows with, they managed to provide a beautiful and decorative homemade wedding cake that another church couple made for us at the last minute! And as the ceremony took place, they played over the speakers the very love song that had now become Marc and I's wedding song, "So Amazing," by Luther Vandross.

The ceremony represented the core of Marc and I – real, intimate, blessed.

A year after we married, we moved to Atlanta together, and the beautiful journey as husband and wife continues to be so amazing.

I am beyond thankful to God for blessing me with the gift of dance because through that gift and through this journey, I found an exceptionally marvelous life partner. I couldn't ask for more.

"As for me and my house, we will serve the LORD."

—Joshua 24:15

Lessons From Mrs. Marvelous

- In God, order and timing can make the journey clear. That's why faith is important. We can easily get discouraged by what we don't see, and confused by what we do see, but when we believe in God's order and God's timing, through faith, we can stay encouraged along our path and be sure of its success.

- A relationship that's spiritually rooted can grow from solid ground.

- The Holy Spirit is real.

- Real love is sacred. Always keep it that way.

Chapter Eight

The Dream: Part 2

So much had transpired for me professionally since my dream to work with Ciara came to fruition in 2008 – from the *I Am...* tour to *OMG*, to working extensively as a back-up dancer for additional R&B and pop artists. But from festival performances overseas to summer tours in the U.S. to award shows and music videos, my work calendar with Ciara remained steady every year since I started dancing with her.

I learned that working consistently with an artist is not something to expect just because you've done a number of projects with them. I saw how variables come into play in this industry that are not in our power as dancers, but entitlement is a sure way to shorten what could've been a promising long journey.

So every time my phone rang for a job, or I received an email or text for work, I was thankful. Because another opportunity for work is not promised nor guaranteed. In realizing my dream, I saw how important strong relationship building is to longevity. Although I had gone on to work for more artists, my relationship with Jamaica and Ciara became strong and that's what ensured the longevity of my working relationship with them.

It had been four years since my last music video shoot with Ciara, and shooting "Body Party," in 2013 for Ciara's fifth album self-titled, *Ciara,* brought me right back to the beginning. Dancing alongside my first bookend in my career – Neo – after not working together for several years, felt just like old times. Ciara and I even did a little skit where she tells me a guy is staring extra hard at me, I ask if he's cute, and then go check him out. The video brought me into the familiar environment I first knew and loved about dancing – grooves, good vibes, and moving to a classic, southern jam by a fellow ATLien.

Shortly after shooting "Body Party," I decided to dye my hair jet black. Four years after first going blonde, I was itching for a change. Because of the style of Ciara's new project, rocking short dark hair still fit with the 90's vibe her project was giving, so the look was well received by the team.

There was a need to find a bookend that was available to dance with me, and during the process of finding and hiring dancers for Ciara, I'd become the designated assistant to teach Jamaica's choreography to them. It was a new role for me – a position of leadership that I hadn't expected – but becoming Ciara's dance captain was an full circle honor because she and Jamaica were the inspiration behind the beginning of this journey.

"I'm Out," featuring Nicki Minaj, became Ciara's second single that year, and we were slated to shoot the music video in Brooklyn in June.

A few months prior, I had taught a masterclass for the first time in my hometown. The choreographers who coordinated the class, Sakinah LeStage and Kiki Ely, were looking to give a scholarship to one participant for use at their upcoming dance convention, *AtLA*. The recipient of the scholarship was based on my selection.

I remember watching one particular dancer that had so much fire and energy when she danced, I couldn't take my eyes off her. I knew there was something special about Jasmine Harper.

I recommended her to Jamaica for consideration as my bookend for Ciara. Jasmine's stunning look and gift and passion for dance spoke for itself, so they loved her. I proceeded to teach her all of the routines from Ciara's catalogue in preparation for the upcoming shows on the calendar. A few weeks later, we found out she would be competing in season ten of *So You Think You Can Dance,* but she was still available to shoot the music video for "I'm Out."

Out of twenty finalists, Jasmine went on to become the runner-up of *So You Think You Can Dance* and a few years later, she and I would get the opportunity to tour together on the *Formation* World Tour. Her success filled me so much happiness and pride.

It was gratifying to have the opportunity to recommend someone with great talent for a job. It's how we all get our start in this industry. Someone giving us a chance. I anticipated the chance to do it more.

2014 had become a pivotal year for me personally, and apparently for Ciara as well, because at the top of the year, she announced that she was pregnant. I was over-the-moon ecstatic for her. By now, even though I revered Ciara as one of my employers, I also looked at her as a friend.

I was working alongside the very woman who inspired the course of my life professionally, who I'd watch evolve year after year, and it was admirable to watch her embrace, so effortlessly, her new role as a mother. We had show dates on the calendar up until she was seven months pregnant, and she still performed seamlessly. Anyone who's seen a Ciara performance knows how high energy and full-out the show is, so I was wowed by her continual tenacity.

As my work calendar for Ciara briefly paused, Jamaica hired me to dance for Grammy Award winning singer/songwriter, NeYo.

This had been years in the making, but the opportunity had finally presented itself for me to be a part of NeYo's incredible team.

I had always been a fan of his music, and when I met him for the first time, he embraced me like we were family. That was the tone his entire team had. It made such an impression on me and made it a joy to work with him. With NeYo, I got to perform in countries I hadn't been to before like Manila, Philippines and the "Las Vegas of Asia," Macau, China.

Macau, China was a special trip for me because there I bungee jumped for the first time. The Macau Tower is the location of the world's highest bungee jump – a 762-foot freefall. Standing at the edge of the tower and realizing what I was about to do as the guide counted down for me to jump was the craziest feeling I had ever experienced. I have no fear of heights, but I'd also never fallen from the sky and at such a high level.

When I tell you that freefall was the most liberating feeling I had ever experienced, I'm not exaggerating. It was such a powerful reminder that the hardest thing for us to do sometimes is to simply surrender and let go. When I took a deep breath and spread my arms wide as I closed my eyes and leaned over the tower, there was such a peace that came over me that surpassed any fear I might've had. The fall happens so fast, but to hear the soft whisper of the wind was such a beautiful moment of serenity.

It was memories like this that has kept me in constant gratitude, because I dreamed and imagined this life I wanted to live. On top of the realization of those dreams, God opened more doors that deepened the journey, and inspired me more.

I was thoroughly enjoying working for NeYo, and in December of 2014, I shot my first music video with him for a single off of his upcoming album, *Non-Fiction*.

The perks of shooting a music video in California means you can shoot a summer video, at the beach, in the winter. "Coming with You," was filmed in Ventura, CA at the Ventura Pier and shooting this video was a genuine good time. Even though I'd come down with bronchitis and had no speaking voice, I made it through as I walked the runway on set, freestyled, and performed choreography in the sand. It was one of the best shoots I'd experienced.

While working for NeYo, I started to dance for Australian rapper, Iggy Azalea.

Working for Iggy produced another full circle experience for me because her choreographer was an Atlanta-based talent named Victor Jackson. Victor, along with my friend Chi-Chi, had taught me how to dance in heels many years before I'd booked my first job. We hadn't crossed paths since I'd started working, so to cross paths almost nine years later was incredibly sweet.

Iggy was hot on the scene, so we were travelling as far as Dubai for shows, doing awards shows like *The American Music Awards*, and touring on iHeart Radio's Jingle Ball throughout 2014. Since the *OMG* tour, I hadn't brought in the new year on stage, but New Year's Eve 2014, I was in Las Vegas dancing on stage as 2015 rang in.

At the top of 2015, my husband was still working steadily with Usher, and I was working with NeYo and Iggy Azalea respectively. We were living comfortably in Los Angeles, but I was greatly missing home.

Being away from family for so many extended periods of time was starting to take its toll on me. Living in Los Angeles meant if I wasn't rehearsing or performing in Atlanta, I was visiting home only on holidays. It was becoming a dream for me to be back in Atlanta so that I could be close to family again.

As husband and wife, any relocating would have to be a mutual decision between Marc and I. Seeming to read my mind, Marc brought up the idea that we consider moving to Atlanta. That was all I needed to hear. I wasted no time getting it from a point of consideration to actualization. As much as I had enjoyed the perks of living in Los Angeles, I was so relieved to know I would be Atlanta based again.

Just as we were preparing to make the big move, I got booked to go on a U.S. tour with Ciara.

It was spring of 2015, and a year after giving birth, Ciara was releasing a new album titled, *Jackie*. Of course, I was happy to be dancing with her again, and after working together on and off over the course of seven years, I would join her on the *Jackie* Tour.

We only had two weeks of rehearsals for tour and rehearsals involved original choreography and learning new choreography. The original dancer that was hired as my bookend had injured herself just before we were slated to hit the road, so the dancer that ended up on tour along with me only had a day and a half to learn sixteen routines.

Lilly Leithner was a dancer from Austria who had short blonde hair like me, so it was dope to have a bookend with a similar look, but still her own unique style. For her to have to learn so many routines in such a short amount of time and pull it off successfully made me respect her greatly. It's not easy to get thrown into a job, dance full out for ninety minutes, remember all of the choreography, remember your entrances and exits, and also be cognitive of performing as if these thoughts are not circulating in your mind. Professionalism is what that's called.

We had a great time working together on the *Jackie* Tour, and eighteen shows in a month meant there were more work days than days off. But there's nothing like working in a positive environment, and working for an artist filled with humility who just simply and effortlessly enjoys what she does.

I've been so fortunate to work for a number of artists whose hearts are so huge and their passion for what they do so strong, but throughout their successes, they remain humble. I think humility comes from knowing that as we live in the reality of our dreams, we realize that end goal as a result of the love, acceptance, and contributions of the people who cross our paths.

Jamaica, who I've affectionately called my "career angel," kept me busy throughout 2015 by hiring me for Ciara and NeYo in the same year. By October of that year, just shy of my 29th birthday, Jamaica also directly booked me to dance in an episode of the hit television drama, *Empire*.

To have an extensive working relationship with Jamaica made my journey in dance that much sweeter. Not only because she greatly inspired me with her talent and style, but her heart and passion creatively, and her humility and compassion towards people also made lasting impressions. She may not hold a lot of auditions for dancers, but she has an eye for special talent and once you work with Jamaica, she uses you for the long-term.

Jamaica has shown me loyalty unparalleled in the industry. And every time I work with her on a job, I am happy and I am grateful.

Following the filming of *Empire,* I continued a few shows with Ciara, and then received a call from one of the choreographers I'd worked with for the *Jackie* tour.

Rhapsody James was a respected choreographer from New York that had come in during tour rehearsals to teach a routine to Ciara's single, "Dance Like We're Making Love". She was now assisting famed dancer/choreographer, Laurie Ann Gibson, for an upcoming performance in New York for Queens rapper, Nicki Minaj, and was checking my availability.

Three years prior, I had worked with Laurie Ann Gibson to dance with Nicki Minaj for the *2012 BET Awards.* I was looking forward to the opportunity to work with both Rhapsody and Laurie Ann again, so I accepted the job and started a day of rehearsals in Los Angeles before flying into New York to continue more.

Lo and behold, Nicki Minaj's performance was a collaboration with Beyoncé and her dancers. At the first rehearsals in New York, I was reunited with Chris Grant, Ashley Everett, and Kimberly Gipson from the *I Am…World Tour.* The last time I'd worked with Beyoncé was in October 2012 for a brief performance at the Barclay's Center in Brooklyn. Three years later, I was back at the Barclay's Center sharing the stage with two women at the top of their respective fields in entertainment.

In December 2015, two months after the performance for Nicki Minaj, I got a call from Chris Grant who wanted to hire me to shoot a music video in New Orleans. For Beyoncé.

I witnessed the payoff of working hard and believing in my dreams and I witnessed the payoff in the lives of the choreographers and artists I've worked with along the way.

We never know at the beginning of the story where the story will end up, but the journey's unfolding is quite the beautiful one.

Lessons From The Dream: Part 2

- Loyalty in the entertainment industry is present.
- In addition to talent, faith, and a strong work ethic, relationships are key to success.
- In the beginning of our respective journeys, people cross our paths for reasons and seasons, and as we grow, those paths can cross again in greater dynamics.
- Family and the presence of familiarity can be a conduit of
- balance to a fast-paced work environment.
- One dream alone can be the inspiration that drives someone along a path of longevity.
- Trust the journey of a dream as it unfolds.

Chapter Nine

Tour Life

THIS IS THE CHAPTER where I get very blunt and real for all of the aspiring dancers that picked up this book. This chapter is to educate people who are not in the entertainment industry about what really goes on, especially on tours. Now some things that you hear may be true, but there are a lot of things that people aren't aware of, and those unknown facts encompass the majority of what goes on when touring with an artist.

This is where I disappoint a lot of you who think that tour life is one big party. It's not. There are definitely great times, but there are equally some not so glorifying moments. From travel days, to call times, to show day schedules, to the physical toll on our bodies, to physical illness, to food poisoning, to checking in and out of various hotels, to long distance relationships and extensive periods away from family and friends, to wardrobe fittings and malfunctions – this is the tour life.

I'm going to give you the real that you don't know about. And to a certain degree, it's good that you don't know about certain things because that means that we were doing our job. Regardless of what goes on offstage, when we're onstage, we're *on*. You'll never see the backstage chaos on stage. At least, you're not supposed to. But this is a very real account of the day-to-day life of a dancer on tour.

First thing to know, pack light. When living out of a suitcase, you want to live out of very few and very light ones. When I first went on the road in 2008, I took seven suitcases. No exaggeration. And this was a job where the dancers weren't responsible for carrying our own wardrobe. I did NOT need to pack a separate bag for every need. When I loaded my things on the tour bus, I was the only one with SEVEN bags for a two-month road trip.

I had a bag for my shoes. A bag for my clothes. Well, four bags for clothes and shoes. A bag for my toiletries. A bag for my snacks. And a bag for miscellaneous items like books, my laptop, camera, pictures. It seemed like I tried to bring my whole house with me on tour.

When we made it back to Atlanta for a break, I knew I had some serious condensing to do. So, instead of seven, I came back on tour with one huge, heavy, bright blue suitcase. It was ridiculous how big and loud this suitcase was, but I fit everything in it.

You can imagine how little space I had for myself and my suitcase in a hotel room. Now add two double beds and another dancer and their belongings, and you can see how cramped the rooms were. It wasn't until the *I Am...*World Tour that I experienced having my own room on the road. With the exception of two occasions, from then on, it became standard for me to have a single room.

Sharing a room on the road is not the most ideal experience. Much like sharing a college dorm room, it can be uncomfortable when you just want to be in your own space and unwind and relax after a show. It's especially hard when sharing a room with someone when you're in a relationship, because once you get to the hotel, it's conversation time with the boo.

But you have to be mindful of the other person in the room because maybe they want to go to sleep. Although you may want to be comfortably relaxing on your bed, yapping away, the conversation may have to go in the hallway, stairway, and sometimes the hotel lobby. However, you may or may not have considerate roommates.

With sharing rooms on the road, it's all about compromise and handling the shared space in a courteous way. You have to share the stage and your living space with this person and you want it to be a positive and enjoyable experience, so approach every scenario with that in mind.

Airplanes. Charter planes. Private jets. Helicopters. Tour buses. Charter buses. Cargo vans. Trains. I've used all these methods of transportation to travel to a show. Sometimes, multiple methods in the same day.

On one of my first tours, we traveled for three weeks in a 12-passenger cargo van as our means of transportation to every show. One trip took seventeen hours straight. It was cramped and crowded with loads of luggage in the first two rows and the entire team in the last two rows, but we had a good time and plenty to laugh about. Don't get it twisted – the artist was in the van right alongside us.

We were the opening act for New Kids on the Block, and that was the type of budget this artist had to work with. You gotta do what you gotta do. But it was a great time. Tami Chynn was the spunkiest artist I've ever had the pleasure of working with. She was equally humble and hungry to realize her dreams. Always smiling and laughing.

For the Australian leg of the *OMG* tour, there was no tour bus, so we had to fly into *every* city. Sometimes, we flew in the day of the show, checked into the hotel, and headed straight to the venue. We'd check out the following morning, and get on another flight to the next city. The next city may have been a show day as well.

Even if we flew into the next city and there was no show, airport travel is very draining when you're physically tired. Your body is naturally dehydrated from the air pressure on the flight, so sometimes our bodies felt like crap. In between shows, our bodies needed time to recover, but there was no sufficient recovery period because we were always preparing to leave for the next flight. It's part of the business, and you gotta make it work to the best of your ability.

Ultimately, touring is all about time management. You have to balance time and attention to your family, friends, and significant other back home, time for yourself, time for your body to recuperate, time to eat, time to sleep, time to sightsee, have fun, and take in all the beautiful places you visit, time for physical exercise and spiritual exercise, and time for personal and professional business matters. There are so many things to think about and do. It's all about making the time you have work for you.

Tour buses are great. They become a home away from home. Most are equipped with twelve bunks, so each individual has their own bunk. There's also a bathroom, kitchen, front and back living area, Wi-Fi, and television. I've never experienced feeling like everyone on the tour bus was on top of each other. Everyone I've been on a tour bus with got along well, so there were no real issues. Some people are more neat than others, but again, it's about compromise and being courteous to one another.

After falling asleep in the bunk for a period of time and then waking up to check in to a hotel is usually when everyone's the most groggy. Something about those bunks put you into a deep sleep. So to wake up to someone yelling, "We're here!" and you're dog tired and then you have to get off the bus, lug your suitcase into the hotel, and stand in line to get your hotel key – it's not the time when everyone's chatty. When it's over an eight-hour trip, oh you better believe everyone's knocked out in their bunks! The life of tour!

And then there's the NUMBER ONE RULE of tour bus etiquette. Absolutely, *no* bowel movement on the bus. Sorry. That has to wait until arriving at the hotel or venue or until the bus driver has a rest stop at a service station.

Here's some more etiquette for aspiring dancers – be kind to the drivers. They work hard, making sure you get to the next city safe and sound, and sometimes they're driving for very long hours. European tour buses usually have two drivers to break up the travel time from one country to the next, but in the States, I've only been on tour buses that had one driver for all the trips. Standard courtesy is for everyone on the bus to pitch in to tip the driver at the end of the tour.

Call time! Call times are the reason you're setting your alarm clock every day. Multiple alarms. When you're on tour, there's no such thing as not setting your alarm clock except for off days that aren't travel days. Your call time is when you're to report to the lobby of your hotel to either check out, head to the venue, or sometimes both. It is what we live by on tour. Everything is on a schedule and it's usually a tight one.

On a typical show day, if we have to check out of the hotel, our lobby call is 10 a.m. If we're staying in the hotel overnight, our lobby call can be as late as 2 p.m. You head to the venue, head to your dressing room, and report to stage for sound check.

For the *OMG* tour, we had the unique experience of performing sound check in front of a select group of fans that paid for the concert packages. Sound check was typically around 5p.m. The artist checks for the levels in their mic, along with the sound of the music and the band, and the band is fine-tuning their instruments and warming up for that evening's show.

During sound check, the dancers aren't sitting around chilling. We're warming up, rehearsing, and cleaning up choreography for the evening's show. Then, dinner is available in catering, so typically after sound check, we all eat at 6-6:30 p.m. Doors open at 7 p.m. The main act is slated to begin around 8:45 p.m. So usually, we're at the venue six hours prior to show time. By the time we leave the venue, we'd have been there for about twelve hours, sometimes longer.

After the show, maybe there's an after party, maybe there's not. We take showers at the venue if we're heading to the next city immediately following the show, or we head back to our hotels for either another show day, a travel day, or an off day.

For women, wardrobe changes during a show are NOT an easy task. It's a madhouse in the quick change. The quick change is a small tent behind the stage where the artist, male dancers, and female dancers have their own respective space to freshen up and change wardrobe for a number or set of numbers. There's one quick change for the artist, one for the female dancers, and one for the male dancers. Beside the artist's, I believe the female dancers' quick change is the most maddening! I want a touring male dancer to argue with me otherwise.

The most wardrobe changes I've had for a show were eight – eight, head-to-toe wardrobe changes. There were three additional jacket on/off moments. This was for the *OMG* Tour. I would like to think that we made it look completely effortless on stage. Offstage, we're panting. We're sweating. But you can't be frantic. Quick changes and frantic don't mix well. Sometimes the changes had to be very swift in order to make it back on stage in time, but the more calm you are, the more efficient the quick change. There's a way to move fast, but be calm at the same time.

As women, we're also trying to keep our hair and makeup looking flawless, so in between changing ever so quickly before the next number requires our presence on stage, we're trying to fix our hair and makeup from the sweat and movement of the numbers prior. It's a lot! But it's quite the rush.

After a while, you find a workable system, but I've been in quick changes where there was one mirror for two dancers, two mirrors for four dancers, and best of all four mirrors for four dancers. You need a smooth-flowing system when girls are a sharing a mirror!

I've been sick on the road before. Sharing close living quarters with a group of people makes room for plenty of colds to go around. On top of that, there are climate changes because one city might've had clear, sunny skies, but in the next, it's cold and raining. It's part of the experience, and another reason it's so important to take care of our bodies on tour.

You become best friends with Vitamin C and Echinacea. There's been a time or two when I didn't keep in touch with my best friends, and one person's sniffles led to mine. It spreads like dominoes! Your goal is to avoid it because sometimes, every week, a new person is coming down with a cold. And Mommy is not there to serve you chicken broth and put a hot rag on your head.

Thank God, I've never had food poisoning on tour, but I've been around plenty people that have. It can easily happen, eating so many different foods from different countries, so it's important to be careful of what you eat around the world. Seafood was always the culprit of food poisoning on tour.

Moving on to long distance relationships. Whew. A long distance relationship on tour is a daunting situation – at least from my experiences. It takes a *very* secure person to handle being with someone while they're away for an extended period of time on tour. A lot of ideas can circulate in your head as to what your partner is up to as they travel the world. While some people may step outside of their relationship to get what they want or feel they need, it's for you to know that your partner is trustworthy and would treat you with the same level of respect they expect to be treated with.

It's about compromise, patience, communication, and understanding. And once again, a balancing act.

The Internet becomes important, especially in foreign countries where talking on your cell phone is financial suicide. Facetime, What's App, Skype, and emails are all great means of communicating with your partner. Unfortunately, Internet is NOT always free in the hotels on tour. Most times, tour management is able to get you complimentary Wi-Fi. Other times, you're paying for Wi-Fi usage. Sometimes, it's a sacrifice. For one day of usage overseas, you may be paying $20, but if you really want to speak to your boo, you're going to charge it to the game, and say thank you to your *per diem*.

The last topic I'm going to discuss is the infamous VIP after-parties. You want to know what it's like? It can be a hit or miss experience. Most after-parties are a great time. Others can be more frustrating than they are fun. It all depends on the city you're in, the atmosphere of the club, the music the DJ spins, the sponsors, the coordinators of the VIP section, the people in the VIP section, and your decision to either stay in the VIP if it gets too crowded or have a good time with fans and friends on the dance floor.

Most of the time, VIP sections are unnecessarily crowded and there's an additional number of people trying to get in and get close to whatever celebrity is in the VIP. It's overrated.

Although the dancers are always invited to the after-parties, we're usually the first ones there as the "entourage". At times, we may have to wait until our boss arrives before the festivities begin. Being a woman on tour with a male entertainer is also a totally different VIP experience from being on tour with a female entertainer.

A lot of times, dancers prefer mingling on the dance floor although there's a chance of getting bum-rushed by fans.

I've been to my share of after-parties and I've never experienced anything extremely wild. They've usually been handled with class. Except for the clan of men and women that cling to the VIP rope anticipating getting in, resulting in forty people occupying a space meant for twenty, after-parties are fun.

After-parties are also a time for roadies to enjoy the company of fellow tour mates and mingle outside of the tour bus, venue, or hotel where we spend majority of our time. Although after-parties can seem redundant, the club, the people you go with, and the music make it a different experience, especially in foreign countries.

Life is ultimately what you make it. When touring, there are so many beautiful places to see, people to meet, things to do, cultures to learn about, and an overall global and human appreciation to gain. When you tour, especially the world, there's so much to take in, not just about other people, races, and cultures, but about yourself and the experience itself. It's all about being fully present to the moment, and also managing your time wisely because tours don't last forever.

I find journaling, taking pictures, and also video blogging to be great tools for capturing the experiences on tour. When you look back on it all, it can fuel a deeper sense of gratitude for having experienced the tour life.

Lessons From The Tour Life

- Balance, organization, and time management are key being on tour. There will be a lot to do both professionally and personally, but once you have an understanding of your work schedule, it's all about how you manage your down time.

- If you want to be productive while on tour, you will have to establish boundaries.

- Capture as many moments as possible, because they're not only priceless to experience in the now, but are beautiful sources of reflection and revelation later.

Chapter Ten

Dream Nuggets

My Dream Outline

At the beginning of this book, I emphasized why creating a vision board can be so powerful in the manifestation of your dreams. But another very helpful tool you can use to organize your visions, is to create a dream outline.

The very first words I started this book with were, "Write the vision and make it plain." In addition to having visual images that reflect my dreams, writing down my dreams and goals has helped me actualize them in so many ways! I pretty much write down everything, but writing is such a great way to also keep track of your thoughts and the goals you have set for yourself.

It keeps you accountable, especially if you write something like, "By this time next year, my financed car will be completely paid off." If you look back at that sentence a year later and your car is not completely paid off, you have to ask yourself what happened throughout the year that prevented you from actualizing your goal. Did you write down your objectives to get your car paid off? Did you create a vision board that complemented the goal you set for yourself? Did you complete the tasks you set for yourself? Did you set any tasks and objectives at all?

Sometimes, goals don't get accomplished because we lose focus for one reason or another. Even though you may not 100% know the exact source that will bring about the realization of your dream, there's no excuse for not planning for how you want to move forward in executing your goals, and ultimately reaching your dream.

That's where your focus comes from. It's all energy. As you continually put energy out toward your dream, you will surely receive energy back for your dream. What you put out, you get in. And I've found that the energy you receive usually exceeds the energy you initially contributed.

But you've got to be self-motivated and get the ball rolling yourself. To help you create your own personal dream outline that you'll hopefully write in your personal journal or notebook, I've created a sample Dream

Outline. This one is based on someone who dreams of becoming a professional dancer and one of their goals is to dance for, as an example, a major artist named Star. Feel free to replace the name Star with your ideal artist. Here is how you would construct an outline to organize how you focus your time and energy:

Sample Dream Outline

"What is my dream?"
MY DREAM is to be a professional dancer
"What is my goal for this dream?"
MY GOAL is to dance for Star
"What are my objectives to achieve my goal & fulfill my dream?"

My Objectives

- *Take dance classes*
- *Take classes and workshops from Star's choreographers*
- *Audition for Star in person*
- *(What are my daily or weekly tasks that will help me complete my objectives so I can accomplish my goal and fulfill my dream?)*

My Tasks

- *Have a few options for audition clothes set aside that would match the look for Star*
- *(based on music, performance, and video footage)*

- *Research Star's choreographers and follow them on social media to stay abreast of any classes, workshops, or auditions they may have*

- *If available, purchase and watch all of Star's concert and tour DVDs*

- *Practice, practice, practice.*

- *Have dance sessions with dance friends*

This is just a sample outline, but the important thing I want you to take away from it is to place checkboxes next to each of your objectives and tasks so that you can check them off as you complete them.

Also, keep in mind that dreams do manifest as a result of your goals. Someone's dream may be to change the world and their goal could be to become President of the United States. Your goals are like platforms to fulfilling your dream. You may fulfill your dream through one platform or another. But focusing on one, clear-cut goal causes you to invest energy into that dream.

There may be a platform that arrives that was different from your initial goal. But that platform may be a part of sowing your seed to accomplishing your ultimate goal. But you have to take it one step at a time. And the first step is setting your intention. Second step, focus. Third step, visualize. And finally, actualize. Believe that your hard work will pay off. Remember, once you get to the second step, you're halfway there!

Nuggets

In addition to sharing my dream outline process, I also want to share some nuggets that I learned along the journey to my dream. Although they are related to dance, they can be applicable to whatever realm your dream is in.

Know Your Worth / Harness Your Power

Rule #1: Don't ever be afraid to say no.

In this industry particularly, you should honor your integrity and morals when it comes to making decisions. Being a people pleaser does not benefit anyone but the person you're inclining yourself to please. Saying no takes courage and strength. There's a fine line between respecting authority and respecting yourself. Because sometimes those in authoritative or higher positions will attempt to use their power to coerce, manipulate, or undercut you. When it comes to making an important decision, it's up to you to discern for yourself what decision is best for you.

A huge, misleading notion in the dance world, particularly as it relates to music artists, is the idea to take *every* opportunity offered to you. As dancers, we must say yes to everything no matter the pay grade, no matter the moral compromise, no matter the hazardous sacrifice to our physical bodies, because how dare we be a dancer and say no to an opportunity.

Especially today, when social media is hugely popular and the 24/7 accessibility to the whereabouts and whatabouts of people is readily available, competition in the dance world expands. Because now, talent can be scouted easily through social media from video posts and pictures.

But the integrity of the art gets a little downgraded because some are willing to do any and everything to be a part of a name or a squad, to acquire the bragging rights to say, "I've done it, too." At what cost have you "done it, too"? As they say, the quicker you rise the harder you fall.

As a community, we have to be conscious of the choices we make. Some opportunities may look like a once in a lifetime situation, but if your impulse precedes logic, the consequences of your decision can be impactful long-term. The same goes for saying yes and saying no. Every decision has a "consequence."

Finances are a very touchy topic, but also a life necessity. Finance is a powerful component in business. For dancers, there is an ignorance when it comes finances, because we tend not to think about the business aspect of a dance career. However, understanding all aspects of the business is necessary to harnessing your power and demanding your worth.

To have a career in dance is to have a passion and love for dance. It is raw, it is emotional, it is feeling, it is heart, it is soul, it is freedom. Finances are not tied to the decision of being a professional dancer. But finances are the only way to economically survive.

Our pay determines our worth in a business. When someone offers you less than you know your worth to be, it's your right to say no.

There's a certain level of prestige associated with each business. Some commercial brands are more popular and therefore have higher revenue than other commercial brands. The same is applicable to music artists. There are some artists that are huge, household names. You know when you see their tour or concert, the cost of tickets is based on the level of worth and value of the show. Higher class of name, higher budget, higher costs.

Being hired to dance for a prestigious artist is indeed an honor. It says your talents and abilities are compatible with this artist and your talent and abilities are desired and worthy of taking a position on the stage with them. For a performance artist, that is honorable. However, that doesn't prevent people from undercutting performers. To be undercut means this business or company finds you replaceable. You don't want to be in a position to be replaceable, so know your strengths, and strengthen your weaknesses.

I say all this to say, do not be afraid to identify, establish, and honor your worth. You can only be your best you. And your best is irreplaceable to the right company. Seek that which honors the greatness in you.

If I believe strongly about a matter, then I will stand up for myself and not be ashamed or made to feel guilty for holding on to my truth.

And fellow young women, please take heed. With all the social pressures and influences in media that display being linked with high profile celebrities giving you instant fame and fortune, it looks like the protocol. But I'm here to emphasize that there's a different way and you can be highly successful without going the easy route. Do not compromise yourself under any conditions. No matter someone's status or position of power. Their line of work and status in their career does not define their authority over you in any situation unrelated to business. Period.

Stay Away From Mess

This goes for messy businesses, messy employers, messy employees, messy gossip, messy relationships, messy anything. One thing's for sure, if you're sitting around a group of people and they're talking bad about someone else, chances are, you could be the next target for a roundtable discussion of messiness.

Don't entertain those types of environments. Conversations should be engaging, but not at the expense of someone else's business. It's not good karma and it shows weakness and insecurity.

In any career, being social with your co-workers is status quo. But sometimes hanging with co-workers can be downright draining. And it shouldn't be. If there's any social environment that affects your integrity or your standards, don't feel pressured to engage. There's a way to make peace without sacrificing your peace of mind. Creating events and outings to invite your co-workers to is one way.

Creating boundaries is another way. If for example, you went out with your co-workers for lunch and that same evening there's an outing to the club that everyone wants to go but you, don't feel obligated to go to the club if that's not what you want to do. You went to lunch. That's good enough.

You shouldn't feel obligated to say yes to every invite, especially if you notice the conversations are not topics that you care to engage in. There's nothing wrong with protecting your peace and having integrity. If people want to call you anti-social or talk about you because you don't do all the "cool" things or provide input in discussions you'd rather not be a part of, then so be it. In this industry, it's important to find a happy medium, but you have to decipher what that happy medium is for you.

No one else can put that definition on you. People will talk behind your back – it comes with the territory – especially when you're the new kid on the block. But gossip is a defense mechanism for insecure people. Stay away from it, because you wouldn't like for people to say false, mean, or vindictive things about you. It doesn't benefit the people engaging in miniscule talk, and it doesn't benefit the person being talked about.

I bring up this particular "nugget" because I've seen firsthand how rumors and talking about people affects relationships and in an unhealthy way. If you're going to talk about other people, you better be very familiar with the circle of people you're talking with and don't be surprised if words come back to you that someone else that wasn't present heard you said. Messiness. Stay away from it.

Being a positive factor in any circle is better than being a negative factor. Always try to see the best in people, because that's how we all want to be seen - in our best light. Who are we to judge someone else's choices or decisions when we all have our own individual choices and decisions we've made that we wouldn't want to be judged by?

The world is better and a much more beautiful place without mess. Messy mouths come from a messy mind, which affects the whole of you – mind, body, and spirit. It's that deep and it's that important to stay away from messy talk. As the old saying goes, "If you ain't got nothing nice to say, don't say nothing at all." Character says a lot about a person. What would engaging in mess say about you?

> *"We can make a large horse go wherever we want by means of a small bit in its mouth. And a small rudder makes a huge ship turn wherever the pilot chooses to go, even though the winds are strong. In the same way, the tongue is a small thing that makes grand speeches.*
>
> *But a tiny spark can set a forest on fire. And among all the parts of the body, the tongue is a flame of fire. It is a whole world of wickedness, corrupting your entire body. It can set your whole life on fire, for it is set on fire by hell itself. People can tame all kinds of animals, birds, reptiles and fish, but no one can tame the tongue. It is restless and evil, full of deadly poison. Sometimes it praises our Lord and Father, and sometimes it curses those who have been made in the image of God. And so blessing and cursing come pouring out of the same mouth. Surely, my brothers and sisters, this is not right!*
>
> *Does a spring water bubble out with both fresh water and bitter water? Does a fig tree produce olives, or a grapevine produce figs? No, and you can't draw fresh water from a salty spring."*
>
> —James 3:3-12

Take Every Experience as an Opportunity to Grow

It is not the end of the world when we get turned down or rejected for an opportunity. In the moment, it may feel like it is because we really wanted that opportunity. There's an element to all of us – a microscopic innate characteristic of entitlement, to have what we want. As babies, we pretty much received, to one degree or another, what we wanted.

Not getting what we want is a harsh reality sometimes, but that reality is good for the soul. It's humbling. Because we all live with wanting something that we don't have. Such is life.

What becomes imperative when we experience that moment of exciting hope, to anxious anticipation, to disappointing rejection, is to acknowledge how we feel, because it is real and we shouldn't deny that part of the experience just because it's uncomfortable. Healing, growth, and wisdom follow such experiences and so it's imperative to do yourself the wonderful service of seeing the bigger picture. Yes, you were told no. But don't take it personal. Hard not to, you might say? From now on, try just for kicks to consider every no a blessing. Think of the times in your life, that you can remember when you were told no. Did your world really end? Or was it just a devastating ego bruise? Poor ego didn't get its way. What a blow to our sense of entitlement. But you're still here.

I'm still here. And more than likely, our most valuable growth spurts came after the no.

What a blessing and what a beauty it is to grow. The more we grow, the more we know. The wiser we become. And someone else's no affords you the opportunity to re-discover, re-channel, and re-activate your power because where there is a no, there is a yes. The task is to identify what you just said yes to as a result of that no. You read that right – identify what YOU just said yes to as a result of that no.

We attract each and every one of our experiences and there is something deep inside you that knew you were going to be rejected and there's a reason it happened. The reason resides in the bigger picture. So see the blessing and the beauty in that. It's not the end of the world after a no. It's actually the beginning of a yes. You haven't lost anything because someone had the power to say no to an opportunity for you.

You do realize you gave them the power to say no after all, right? Now you've actually found an opportunity to say yes again to your power. Own it, tap in, and utilize it for the bigger picture in your life. Gratitude is golden, so give thanks for that no, and give thanks in advance for the power within you to say yes to a better you. Have fun discovering and experiencing the new yes that will come as a result of your growth!

Respect The Journey

Life is a lot like traveling. You may know where you want to go, yet give no consideration to the time it takes to get there. One might say, "I would love to go to Africa!" But a flight from New York to South Africa is sixteen hours. That turns a lot of people off. We want to travel, but we don't want it to take sixteen hours to get to our destination. But such is life.

Just because we want something doesn't mean we will get to it in an instant. There's a journey of patience we must tread before arriving at the destination. It may take days, weeks, months, or years, but we will get there if it's what we truly want.

We have to be willing to stretch our wings. There's a whole world out there to explore, but we have to want to reach for it – to step outside of our comfort zone. To wear patience with a smile and be willing to experience the, sometimes grueling, process it takes to get to the place that inspired our journey. You never know what you could discover as you navigate towards your destination. Respect the journey. That is priceless.

"Never underestimate the power of dreams and the influence of the human spirit. We are all the same in this notion: The potential for greatness lives within each of us."

—Wilma Rudolph
(1st American woman 3x
Olympic Gold Medalist)

Chapter Eleven

Formation

I KNEW SOMETHING was different about this job. Something special was taking place and this moment was the predecessor to an unforgettable journey. Arriving in New Orleans in December of 2015, all I knew was I was there to shoot something for what was called, *Project Lemonade*. As soon as I checked in to the hotel, I was swept into the fitting room for wardrobe and shortly after, into a van headed to set. It was a beautiful, cool day and we were shooting near a park that overlooked a river.

The first thing I was asked upon arriving on set was if I knew how to play tug of war. Next thing I knew, I was standing at the bank of the river tied to one end of a rope, with Beyoncé tied to the other end. For a few minutes, we just leaned against each other's weight through the rope and stared into each other's eyes. It was a beautiful moment of connection, trust, and test of strength. I called it the tug of love. And I was honored to share that moment with Beyoncé.

From that scene, I changed into what I called a healing ceremony outfit. I'd never stood knee deep in water with a group of women in a circle before. While the water was undeniably cold, the moment itself was so warm. Holding hands submerged in water from the waist down felt extremely powerful.

Sisterhood, unity, healing, power, forgiveness – those were the words that came to mind as we were shooting that scene. I couldn't believe how magical the day was feeling. And I knew it was a day I wouldn't soon forget. But the day wasn't over.

After a full day on set, there were dance rehearsals waiting for our attendance immediately following. Walking into the gym and seeing about twenty-five girls dancing full out to a new song by Beyoncé got me extremely hyped. The song was very different from anything I had heard her record before and it was gritty. The choreography equally matched the rawness of the song, so I loved everything about it.

Formation was going to slay.

After a magical day and an energetic night, there was more content to shoot the following day. This time, the set was on a plantation. I immediately felt a sense of spiritual purpose. With everything so stripped down – girls wearing their natural hair on set, little to no makeup, and wardrobe inspired by the antebellum south – it was a beautiful sight to see.

The uneasiness of some of the ladies was noticeable, as we are in a climate where social media portrays perfection and with the accessibility of so many filters, one could look like a million bucks at the click of a button. But as the day drew on, the walls came down, the vulnerability didn't feel so intense, and the ladies started to embrace their freedom. How appropriate, because for one of the scenes, Beyoncé sang *acapella* another one of her new songs called "Freedom."

I fell in love with the song the moment she sang the first few words.

> *Tryna rain, tryna rain on this thunder,*
> *tell the storm I'm new,*
> *I'ma walk, I'ma march on the regular,*
> *painting white flags blue.*

In my mind, this sealed the notion that Beyoncé was up to something so powerful, so substantial, so groundbreaking, that all I could do was thank God for blessing me to be a part of this moment. Only once I saw the film premiere of *Lemonade* months later, did I come to understand exactly what all I was shooting for.

Being a part of *Lemonade*, Beyoncé's video film, I was able to directly connect, as a woman, to the chapters she broke the visual album into. A woman goes through various emotional stages – intuition, denial, anger, apathy, emptiness, accountability, reformation, forgiveness, resurrection, hope, redemption – that cultivate and expose our strengths, weaknesses, and power.

I realized the journey of such stages in my own life. How full-circle this was to return to where it all took off for me, seven years later. I was older, wiser, more experienced and mature. With that, I knew this time around, what I was getting ready to experience was going to be more powerful and meaningful than anything I had previously done in my career.

Just like that, on January 9, 2016, it happened. That sudden, drastic change of events. My agent sent the text that I was booked for the Superbowl with Beyoncé. And so it began – as I was dressed to go on stage with Ciara in Arizona, and preparing to travel to Malaysia for Ne-yo a few days later, my life took on a new formation.

There is indeed strength and power in numbers and I could feel it all around me rehearsing alongside thirty other phenomenal dancers for the Superbowl. The entire team worked unrelentingly hard to ensure the highest level of success for this performance, along with Beyoncé's upcoming *Lemonade* film premiere, album release, and the *Formation* World Tour itself.

To be a part of such creative processes and expression, and to see the reality of dreams not just for myself, but for a multitude of people is so deeply gratifying.

That's what *Formation* was about to me.

Seeing how important the common thread is between people – community, collective, collaboration. It takes a team to create and achieve greatness. A team to see results. A team to inspire change. When love is the foundation and excellence the core of a project, there's no room for failure. I knew I was a part of a winning team because Parkwood Entertainment was about love and excellence expressed.

One can't help but be inspired in a room full of passionate, hungry, and dedicated individuals, and no matter how many jobs I've done, it never gets old being a part of new and great creative pursuits. I was ready for this journey and ready to get in formation.

The adrenaline rush knowing we were in rehearsals for a historic Superbowl performance, and in the middle of the process, taking a day out to shoot the music video for "Formation" itself was thrilling. We had late rehearsals the night before the "Formation" video shoot and still had to be on set at 4:45am. By the time we finished shooting the last scene, it was midnight. And we had rehearsals for the Superbowl resuming the following morning.

But the energy on set was amazing. You could feel the magic happening as all of us dressed in matching brown and black Afro wigs and denim outfits for the full cast dance scene. Knowing we were consciously setting a refreshing tone for black women was deeply gratifying.

The poignant statement Beyoncé was making with her newest projects couldn't be denied. Without knowing what the rest of the video would look like, I knew based on the scenes we did that day, the video was going to be the best of the year.

It was an intense process preparing for the Superbowl performance of "Formation" as well as the *Formation* World Tour itself. Every day, there were changes and every day there was new movement and direction to learn. As a dancer, learning the choreography is one process, but formations with the choreography is another. Obviously, with thirty dancers for Superbowl and twenty dancers for tour, "Formation" couldn't be a performance without plenty of formations to accommodate it.

So as the final date to the main event and opening night approaches, changes are inevitable. Formations come and go. Choreography comes and goes. But one thing remains the same. History was in the making. I was working for someone who was doing what had never been done before in entertainment. Beyoncé was performing on the Superbowl with a socio-political message backed by a field of all black women.

The energy between Coldplay, Bruno Mars, and Beyoncé in rehearsals further pushed the positive feelings that what was happening was special. With Coldplay laying the foundation of love, Bruno Mars layering that love with funk and soul, and Beyoncé topping it all off as the messenger for a community who desperately needed to hear and see a strong and loud voice of love, the magic was inevitable.

To perform at the Superbowl twice in a lifetime is an incredible feat. But to know that this particular performance would be among a historic line of prominent, Superbowl performance moments similar to the likes of Whitney Houston, Michael Jackson, Diana Ross, James Brown, and Prince reminded me of why I was so grateful for following my dreams and trusting that God would open doors for me as a professional dancer. There has been no greater feeling in my professional career than to be a part of history.

To be on the field in Santa Clara, California at the Levi's Stadium on February 7, 2016 is a moment in time I will never forget. Superbowl 50 came at a time where social issues were becoming more popular than entertainment itself. With social media being the centerpiece of news and information, incidents occurring in any part of the world immediately became local news.

One of the major social issues that affects my community is police brutality against Blacks, particularly our Black men. While there were people who interpreted our Superbowl performance as a ploy against police, it had absolutely nothing to do with police, and everything to do with empowerment and pride for our community and for women.

I was so thankful to be standing on the front line with Bey as this era served the sweetest recipe for Lemonade. There's nothing like being a conduit for inspiration and we were all sprinkling that black girl magic on the Levi Stadium field for millions around the world to see. We are so much greater than the hate that is projected on us as a result of fear.

When I hit the stage to dance on the *Formation* Tour, there was no fear. I saw a very vivid vision of performing with excellence. Giving my best with every step, every moment of execution, every song. Before I went on stage every night, I prayed. While the fans watched the monolith rotate as the opening interstitial played on its screen, I was thanking God for another opportunity to go on stage and share my passion, my love, and my gratitude for what I do and for where I am.

I thanked God for all of the women I got to perform alongside and asked God to allow the show to be the most successful it could possibly be, that all departments would function as one unit. I prayed that in that moment, for the crew, the band, the Mamas,

Beyoncé, the dancers, and the viewing audience, we would all experience love and joy.

Then, it was show time.

Being on the *Formation* Tour was in perfect alignment with my desire to do purpose work on a job. With the heavy media coverage of police brutality on African-American people in the United States, I had an opportunity to express my pain, my anger, my plea, my faith, my hope, and my love on stage in front of millions of people. I was a part of a tour that gave me the platform to express myself in a meaningful way.

At this point in my life, I saw myself in a way I hadn't seen me quite before. Unapologetically confident, trusting, present, free. For the first time in my career, every move had intent for me. Every song was interwoven into the soundtrack of my own life. I connected with the emotional representations of our show. And it was a blessing to be a part of a show that as a woman, I could relate to.

Music is such beautiful art and serves as the canvas that we paint so many pictures with. With songs like "Formation" and "Freedom", I felt like I was painting the picture of a soldier on the front line. Ready to war for love. Prepared to stand in the gap of reality versus dreams. Ready to show young girls from the north to the south, east and west that black is indeed beautiful, power is beautiful, faith is beautiful, love is beautiful, respect is beautiful, and art is beautiful.

Every song I danced to gave me an outlet for the expression of how I feel today as a woman. When I performed "Freedom," I felt pride for being a strong woman. I felt honored to be a representation of my ancestors. I aspired to invoke raw emotions from the audience.

Performing in water every night felt like a spiritual bath. A cleansing and purifying ritual to close out the energy that was exchanged between us and the audience. I felt vulnerable opening my heart in honest performing, yet I felt free.

There was one particular show in Glasgow, Scotland on the *Formation* tour where the performance of "Freedom" was different from any other night. There had been another major news breakout of an unarmed black man who was fatally shot by a police officer. The energy that day among the team was significantly lower than most days. We were all so emotionally drained and distraught from realizing, yet again, that our brothers were not safe in the streets of America, and the reality of that was shaking all of us to the core.

How many more times would there be a repeat instance of the same tragic headline, "Black man slain by police officer." Same stories, different cities. We were all so sick of it and our hearts were hurting for the families whose lives would never be the same as a result of senseless violence.

A few hours prior to show time, the choreographers announced to the dancers that for the "Freedom" segment of the show, Beyoncé wanted to have a moment of silence for the recent victims of police brutality. It was absolutely appropriate because it was the only thing on all of our minds that day. I couldn't wait to get to "Freedom" tha night, because my emotions were so heavy. "Freedom" was the only opportunity in the show for me to let it all out.

I will never forget standing in the water in complete silence as Beyoncé began to sing "Freedom" *a capella*. The tears…I could hold back no more. I never cried on stage like I had in that moment. From the start of "Freedom" to the finish, I let the tears fall as my hands and feet kicked in the warm water, the movement pouring from the depths of my soul. We were all in complete silence after the show, some of us still choked up from the heavy emotions we'd just released.

This was a show I would never forget.

Preparing for greatness consisted of long rehearsal days and nights. And with my Sister Queens — a term of endearment the tour dancers used to describe each other — late night outings, laughs, dancing, allowing our walls to come down, and lifting each other up in love added a unique richness to the experience.

When the heart posture of creative vision is centered in love and harmony, there is a beautiful formation of light on display in the world. And that journey of a dream can only lead to one destination. Freedom.

For ten months, I was surrounded by beautiful, talented, passionate, extraordinary beings capable of affecting the world and each other. I was also learning once again from the very woman who completely changed my world as I knew it, seven years ago. How full circle it felt to be right back where it all started for me, and to witness and support Beyoncé doing what only she can do best on an even bigger scale.

I couldn't have predicted that the end of my dance journey would be in *Formation*. But I am so thankful that God saw fit to bless me with experiences in my career that have broadened the scope of my imagination and surrounded me with a legendary artist and team to learn and grow from. May the journey of spiritual formation continue…

Lessons From Formation

- There is strength and power in numbers.
- Unity is of the essence for a successful formation of anything.
- I didn't imagine having the opportunity to tour with Beyoncé again, but I had grown so much throughout my journey, it was a beautiful experience to share my wisdom from over the years with the young women who were touring the world for the first time. Pay it forward.

Acknowledgements

PRAISE AND HONOR TO GOD in Christ Jesus for grace, mercy, favor, and for being my guiding light as I continue to navigate through each journey. For every person that inspires, loves, motivates, and keeps me lifted in prayer, I thank God for you. My husband, Marc, thank you for being the love of my life and my best friend. Your infectious inspiration and tireless love and support of me keeps me going. I thank God so much for you. Mom & Dad, without you, my purpose wouldn't exist. You are the incredible seed sowers that provided the perfect union to my story with your love. I thank you for being my greatest teachers and motivators, and being my first introduction to unconditional love. I love and honor you both. Ayhanna and DJ, I am beyond blessed to call you my siblings. You are the greatest support and encouragement I could ever ask for. Thank you for being the exceptional souls that you are and for always keeping a smile on my face and inspiring me to reach for my highest potential. To my bonus dad, D, Thank you for cultivating my work ethic and determination at a very young age and for always seeing the champion in me. It was because of you that I understood the principle of visualization and pushing past any perceived limits. I'll never forget, I can do ALL things through Christ who strengthens me. Juicy, thank you for the undeniable joy you've brought to my life since the moment you came in it. I love you babygirl. Aris, you knew we would make a successful team. Thank you for believing in me before I had anything to show for it and thank you for being in my corner through some of the toughest decisions I had to make in my journey. You have stood by me through it all!! To the best superagent I know, I love you and will always be Team Xcel! Jamaica Craft, my career angel. The Queen of Sauce. You. Are. The reason. Thank you for all that you are and all that you do. You have touched my life beyond the steps, have been in my corner from day one, and I am so grateful to know you and for the blessing that is you. I love you sis. Ciara, you are a real gem in my life. Thank you for being so loyal to me over the years, for supporting me and embracing me as family. The light of God is so reflective in you and your journey and I am so thankful to have witnessed your growth up close and personal over the years. Love you always CiCi! Tiffany, Jetaime, Shaquasha, and Cekoya, my best friends and Sister Queens in Christ! Thank you for being my warriors in life, love, prayer, and truth. For holding me down in the realest way throughout my journey and beyond! I couldn't ask for a greater friendship and sisterhood than the one we have! I love ya'll twice! Donald, Clifton, and Byrd, from Couture to HipHopcrisy, you are the day ones who encouraged and pushed me to go for my dream and make it happen. God knew what He was doing when our paths met and I am so thankful for the humbled beginnings and cherished memories we forever share! I love you deeply. My Impact Center Church family, you all light up my life and I thank God for the fellowship and community I have in you! Thank you for keeping me lifted in love and prayer! Pastor Jon McKinney and First Lady J, I love you to the moon! My Spirit Food Christian Center family, thank you for being home away from home and for the many years of fellowship, accountability, love, and support! Pastor Z and First Lady Antonia, thank you for your guidance and love!

Beyoncé, thank you for bringing out the best in me. You showed me, in many ways, my capability and strength as a woman and to be the leader I was always called to be. For challenging and inspiring me in the most gentle, but fierce way to harness my own power, you are a Godsend. And thank you Queen, for your support of this book! Yvette and Melissa, Thank you. Thank you. Thank you. My incredible Tour Families, from *I Am* to *OMG* to *Compound Entertainment* to *Jackie* to *Formation,* Thank you to the artists, management, staff, crew, musicians, dancers, and choreographers for propelling my growth as a performer and a woman. I have gone to the best school in the industry because I learned so much from being surrounded by the best of the best in the game. Thank you all for being exceptional at what you do and for inspiring me greatly. Chyna, you were the first to review my book, and I thank you for being a strong anchor and crucial support in the self-publishing of it! Sherri Lewis, I couldn't have published this book without you! Thank you for being the best editor I could hope for, and for your sincere transparency and support! Reyna, Sis, thank you for rallying for me to complete this book and for being such an amazing prayer warrior, sister, and friend in my life! You are so powerfully anointed! I love you!

To my extraordinary fans, you hold me up in a way I never imagined I could be when I started this journey. You all have sent outpours of love time and time again and I am blessed to have an extended family and community in you. I appreciate you all and trust that this book offered the greatest insight to the journey you have followed me on for so long! Let's continue to grow together! Love you TeamSaidah!